D0252368

THE

MONK

AND THE

SKEPTIC

THE

MONK

AND THE

SKEPTIC

Dialogues on Sex, Faith, and Religion

FRANK BROWNING

SOFT SKULL PRESS
An Imprint of Counterpoint

Copyright © 2013 Frank Browning

All rights reserved under International and Pan-American Copyright Conventions. No part of this book may be used or reproduced in any manner whatsoever without written permission from the publisher, except in the case of brief quotations embodied in critical articles and reviews.

Though formally others in the Dominican Order referred to Peter, an ordained priest, as Father, that term didn't seem quite right for our relationship, so I refer to him as *Brother Peter.*

Library of Congress Cataloging-in-Publication Data

Browning, Frank, 1946-
The monk & the skeptic : dialogues on sex, faith, and religion / Frank Browning.
    pages cm
ISBN 978-1-61902-183-9
1. Sex—Religious aspects—Christianity. I. Title. II. Title: Monk and the skeptic.

BT708.B79 2013
261.8'357—dc23

                        2013014417
ISBN 978–1–61902–183-9

Cover design by Michel Vrana
Interior design by Domini Dragoone

Soft Skull Press
An Imprint of Counterpoint
1919 Fifth Street
Berkeley, CA 94710
www.softskull.com

Printed in the United States of America
Distributed by Publishers Group West

10 9 8 7 6 5 4 3 2 1

I look on all sides, and everywhere I see nothing but obscurity.
Nature offers me nothing that is not a matter of doubt and disquiet.

If I saw no signs of a divinity, I would fix myself in denial. If I
saw everywhere the marks of a Creator, I would repose peacefully
in faith. But seeing too much to deny Him, and too little to assure
me, I am in a pitiful state, and I would wish a hundred times that
if a god sustains nature it would reveal Him without ambiguity.

—Blaise Pascal, *Pensées*

Contents

CHAPTER ONE

INVITATION TO COMMUNION

In which the inquisitor cruises his first
Holy Father and finds him quick of flesh.

O ur story begins when the two of us are in the Jeu de
Paume gallery on the Place de la Concorde looking at
a new show by Pierre et Gilles, the French photographic artist
whose work wavers between the kitsch and the surreal. We are
standing side by side before an image of Saint Peter, rendered
as a gymnast porn star crucified upside down. I hadn't known
the details of Saint Peter's crucifixion, having had no childhood religious instruction. I draw in my breath in polite shock.
"That's rough," I say to the tallish man standing next to me.

"It's just how they crucified Saint Peter," the man answers.
He is dressed in jeans and a leather jacket. I nod, then turn my

attention back to the painting. I haven't yet noticed the rosary beads hanging from the watch pocket of the gentleman's Levi's.

A moment passes.

"Do you always cruise priests in art galleries?" he asks.

"Only attractive ones," I answer, startled, but eager for a reasonable response.

So our friendship opens on a cold, sunny December afternoon. We stop for a coffee at a nearby café where he—we'll call him Brother Peter—explains that contrary to my expectation he doesn't find the Pierre et Gilles images at all sacrilegious. Moreover, he knows the artists to be practicing Catholics, which leaves me more startled. Before he departs for his daily swim we agree to meet again. Brother Peter's daily swim was as inviolate as his daily hour of silent prayer before he joins his fellow monks. He always dwelt, even in his travels, within a Dominican community.

A few days later we meet for another coffee in my apartment. He lingers for an hour afterward. Our meetings continue over the following several months in one city or another. He is quick to explain that he is not at all available for what is called "a relationship," as he is married in the most profound sense to his spiritual community. Nor I, I answer, since I am completely comfortable in my own decidedly more secular relationship. Our conversations advance, sometimes with physical interludes, surveying, debating, exploring the nature of secular and spiritual friendship; the relation of the body to

God, or gods; the mission of charity enacted by the notorious high-drag Sisters of Perpetual Indulgence, several of whom he has known rather well; the value and the danger of transvestism, which, while he has never tried drag, he appreciates immensely; the biblical interdictions about improper pleasures of the body and how he manages his confessions knowing that he is unlikely to quit having sex with other men; the matter of sinful use of another's body; his unyielding opposition to gay marriage; and his conviction that the human body, and in particular his own body, will persist in its finest perfection for all eternity—so long as he maintains his faith and follows the duties and obligations prescribed by Christ.

We both liked sex. More to the point, we shared a similar sexual sensibility: aside from short-term excitement, we both experienced sex as a route to another kind of knowledge. For me sex has always been a means toward a human connection greater than the thing itself. Even in the anonymous variety in the parks, forests, and undergrounds around Paris, San Francisco, and New York, orgasm, jouissance as the French would have it, has seldom been the point. (Or as an old friend once put it, if it's just about orgasm, he'd rather have a Cuban sandwich.) The acts may be brief and possess no intention or capacity for enduring companionship. What is usually called romance may be utterly out of the question, but what has always been essential is the disarming intimacy of naked touch—knees, nipples, tongues, buttocks, though (almost) never undressed penises. Odd as it may sound, the caress of skin to skin lets loose a calisthenics of rich and complex intimacies, animal and atavistic, unrelated to the mindfulness of romance. Sex for Brother Peter is, he says, never about romance. Certainly it is not about confessions of devotion. It would take several months before I began to comprehend what it was he could bring to sexual acts and what he derived from them.

So far as I know, I had never before lain with a true priest, nor have I since. But it wasn't long after Brother Peter left my apartment that wintry afternoon that I was propelled back more than two decades to an encounter with a magnificently beautiful and tortured young man who had fled from his seminary on the eve of his ordination. I met that man in Elysian Park in downtown Los Angeles. It was late on an autumn afternoon. The sun falling to the west turned the dry grass gold. The man had just dismounted a BMW muscle bike, which I soon learned was his only possession. He was dressed in Levi's and a denim shirt, half buttoned. He hadn't shaved for several days, though the bristle was thin. His eyes were set wide apart, deep and worrisome. I was tending my dog, an Australian shepherd lost in all the fragrances of canine paradise.

The man—Rafe—simply stared at me. Motionless. I pretended to read. He leaned himself against the saddle of his bike and began to stroke his bare and hairless chest. It became obvious that I was not reading. He walked over to me, sat on the same large rock where I was perched, put his arm around my shoulders, and kissed me.

"Can I come home with you?" he asked.

He had not showered in some days, but I agreed. The next morning he asked if he could stay with me.

"Where do you live?" I asked.

"I've been in the park for two weeks. I'm a priest. No, not really. I was supposed to be. I was supposed to be ordained this month. I can't do it." He began to sob. "I don't have anywhere [to go]," he whimpered. "They'll come and get me. Please."

When I got home from work that afternoon, anguished over what to do and how to say it, Rafe was gone without a trace. There are hundreds of stories like Rafe's, maybe thousands. Until I crossed paths with Brother Peter, Rafe had all but disappeared from my memory, but Brother Peter's warm, tactile presence brought Rafe back as though it were with him that I had passed the afternoon. By now he would be the same age as Brother Peter. Calm and at peace as Brother Peter seemed, I would soon learn that his torment in his twenties was every bit as painful as Rafe's had been. His suffering led him to the cusp of self-destruction.

I never heard again from Rafe, and I frequently felt guilty after his disappearance for not having offered him more. That guilt vanished in time, only to resurface in the hours after Brother Peter left. What sort of institution was this church that for all its promise of deliverance from suffering propelled many of its sons to the ledge of oblivion? Was I drawn to this cultured monk only by the titillation of the exotic? Did the one man's success at negotiating the contradictions between his mission and his desire erase the other's desperation at the hands of the same hierarchy? Must I judge? Must I suppress recollection of Rafe's pain (and his very possible self-destruction) in order to continue these sublime afternoons enjoying both the dialogue and the lust that Brother Peter brought?

In an earlier era, when scarcely the only images of homosexuality were to be found on the cracked vases of classical Greece (and most of those hidden away behind brick walls), Rafe would likely have suffered in silent sublimation. Brother Peter would have restricted his engagements to long retreats in distant lands—not that homosexuality was unknown in the cloth. Prior to the twentieth century the priesthood was frequently the natural home for men who simply lacked the means or the libido to claim women for their dowries and the physical relief they offered. Boccaccio's *Decameron* notwithstanding, those who entered the monastic orders were strictly surveilled. Exposure led not merely to defrocking, but also to destitution or death. As recently as half a century ago, there were no models of the happy homo rewarded with public posts as a standard check mark on the diversity chart, and there was scant counseling to reassure homosexual men and women that cocksucking, butt fucking, and cunnilingus were normal, natural sexual activities. In those times I would not have crossed trails with either Rafe or Brother Peter. And even now I wouldn't entertain lifting the cloth of an obvious cleric. Somehow both the abstract notion as well as the image bears too much the incense of kitsch. Robes and dresses, beads and sequins, collars and bondage, sandals and pumps. To seek it out seems too much like a Sacha Baron Cohen version of *Our Lady of the Flowers*. Not to mention the bad odor of rampant priestly child abuse that hangs like an acid cloud from Dublin to Culver City, the images from Buñuel's *Viridiana* with its swinging lamp in the form of a bishop's head, or Torquemada (a Dominican) and the burning of the Jews.

Still, both of these believing Catholics tugged at my curiosity. Raised utterly secular (heathen, one friend said), I was fascinated that they seemed equally anchored in modernity and in the Middle Ages. If for Rafe that duality had proved to be an impossible division, Brother Peter seemed to suffer no anxiety at all. Despite my own lack of religious education, I have never harbored any personal hostility to those who do pursue religion. My father fended off itinerant Kentucky preachers by pulling out a newspaper clipping that he stored inside the Seth Thomas windup clock he kept on his desk. The clipping listed the schedule of Unitarian services in far away Lexington, Kentucky. Unitarians were an unknown species in the countryside and were neither more nor less suspicious than sodomites. The preachers usually skedaddled off in confusion. In fact I doubt that my father had ever attended a Unitarian meeting.

Priests on the other hand were fascinating and mysterious sorts for a boy who went to a two-room school and then scampered up the lane from the school bus into a house filled with thousands of books in multiple languages. Priests spoke Latin. They didn't spit tobacco, or say *hain't* for *hasn't*, or pronounce the capital of Argentina "Boo-ee-nis Airs," as my grade school teacher did. Father Hubert, from Saint Charles in Flemingsburg, Kentucky, was as likely to come out to the farm to buy apples on a Sunday afternoon as was anyone else, while the fire-and-brimstone evangelical sorts condemned business on the Sabbath. He seemed lean and fit beneath his black cassock, his face ruddy-cheeked behind wire-rimmed glasses. If memory serves me correctly, he once engaged my father, who had won himself the college Latin prize, in some sort of banter about Augustine and utopian dreams. And finally, he lived in what I always regarded as the prettiest house in town, a plain, one-story, white building with a tile roof and leaded glass windows bent in French curves. It was said that he drank wine at dinner.

I was shocked to learn decades later about another priest down on the river—the Ohio—who had been sent to the penitentiary for disrobing choirboys and engaging them in cocksucking instruction (however much I might have profited from such expert direction). *Cocksucker* was then merely a dirty word schoolyard boys hurled at each other as a prelude to a fistfight. It was not an imaginable activity. As well, the reality of being a priest was nearly unimaginable. My young classmates were taught in their Sunday schools that priests were the agents of an alien power run from a secret and largely diabolical temple far across the waters and that Catholics were not Christians. In our home such talk was quickly dismissed as rural ignorance about which we should feel charity but say nothing. Yet such liberal enlightenment only intensified the exotic aura surrounding such an impossible creature: a man who talked about the Bible, who knew the Psalms and the Song of Solomon, and who wasn't a stupid hillbilly.

Come puberty and the thrice-daily exercise of right-handed self-relief, the exoticism intensified. Catholic boys, I learned in high school, were admonished by their religious teachers not to touch themselves in that way lest they (a) go blind, (b) become deaf, (c) sprout pubic hair in their palms, or (d) descend into insanity. (Being neither Catholic nor any other sort of Christian, I rejected the first three as nonsense, but seriously wondered about the insanity option until well into my twenties. One heterosexual friend, subjected to Jesuit instruction, told me he had never dared to touch his sexual tools until after he had plunged into his first vagina, so terrified was he of the dark consequences. It must have been then that I began to understand personally the diabolical heritage of the Inquisition (whose chief agents were the Dominican order). How did these athletic young men who took up the cloth manage their impulses? And how could they square their rich education, fully accepting of science, evolution, the Big Bang, with the ludicrous teachings about hairy palms? I longed to ask our county public health director, the community's highest-profile Irish Catholic, such questions. I even imagined a scenario in which his daughter, my coeditor at the high school paper, would invite me to their house where, as she was helping her mom with dinner, I would pose the question. But of course I never dared. Such questions eventually proved merely academic once a real, live penis belonging to another male made its way toward me. The teachings about sex emitted by Holy Mother Church or Her evangelical cousins seemed simply silly by the 1970s.

Once the AIDS plague arrived full throttle by the '80s, church doctrine moved from the anachronistically ludicrous to the morally reprehensible. Masturbation, as Bill Clinton's first surgeon general urged, was the ultimate safe sex—a technique she recommended to all the young or unattached (or even to the attached who sought out more); for that counsel she was fired. Worse yet was to come from a series of scandals that nearly bankrupted the church in Massachusetts and all but destroyed what had been a near ecclesiastical regime for sixty-five years in Ireland. The Irish Catholic priesthood was revealed as possibly the single largest organized brigade of pedophiles in the Western world. No modern republic had been so thoroughly dominated by the Vatican and its emissaries as Ireland. Not only were all the putatively public schools run by the church, but also the 1937 constitution recognized the "special position" of the Holy Roman and Apostolic Church in preserving and protecting the faith of Irish citizens. The acid glare from the priests and nuns at any who challenged church dogma burned like volcanic coals—as I learned while traveling in the '70s with an Irish friend who was a single mother.

Then as the scandals of brutal and buggering priests at last leaked into the national newspapers and eventually state radio, the whole structure imploded. Daily phone-in programs on RTÉ Radio were inundated with calls from men in their forties who broke down sobbing as they recounted having been held after classes and repeatedly raped by pale, pudgy men in their shoe-length black soutanes. Tough working-class grandmas whom I met while reporting on Irish schools lost control of themselves as they recounted the fear they still felt even entering a school building. Mothers in their sixties called the radio to talk about their disappeared sons. And too often some of those sons' skeletons were exhumed from unmarked graves, the beating marks yet visible on their once-young skulls. My old image of my father and Father

Hubert discussing Saint Augustine over sherry was all but obliterated by these ghastly accounts, replaced by a vicious tableau of bitter, mean, violent men beating and raping little boys in the church cloakroom. I could only ask myself, what sort of persons could these men be?

One insight came when I spoke to Marie Keenan, a social worker and psychotherapist at University College Dublin, who had spent more than a decade interviewing priests about their sexual and emotional experience. "These men who are in the seminary can't express themselves, are not encouraged to express themselves, are not helped to know and understand the mechanisms of their body," she told me. "They're out there without support, without supervision, and it is only a matter of time. When you put these men . . . [when] you give them access to children and put them in positions of power, over time their sexual needs will emerge. It's just like the system blows." Richard Sipe, a former Benedictine monk, who has spent his post clerical life exploring the effects of enforced celibacy, was even more outspoken: "As the [U.S. Conference of Catholic] bishops' own study published in 1972 said, two-thirds of priests are either mal-developed or undeveloped psychosexually. Only 20 percent are developing and 10 percent are developed . . . What we are producing [are] emotional thirteen-year-olds."

Little, apparently, has changed since then, either in the United States or Ireland. In France, priests are simply a

disappearing species, while in Italy, where the Vatican continues to weigh heavily on domestic politics, the priests are said
to have long maintained a "special position" for their house-
keepers. Yet officially the teachings of the church regarding
sexuality remain locked in a nether zone that drifts further
and further from science, psychology, common sense, or
real practice. That couldn't be clearer than in the theological
treatment of masturbation or, more correctly, antimasturbation. One of the most extreme arguments comes from a
former Saint Mary's College theologian, E. Michael Jones,
who characterizes masturbation as "the root sexual evil first
of all from a developmental point of view—it is the child's
introduction to sexual sinning—but also because all other
sexual sinning is at its root masturbatory." Jones left Saint
Mary's (in Indiana) because he didn't present a sufficiently
stern Catholic education; afterward he drifted in and out
of Holocaust denial journals. Yet Pope Paul VI, among the
most sober of recent popes, was only slightly softer in his
denunciation of the solitary sin, issued in 1975 via the Sacred
Congregation for the Doctrine of the Faith: "Masturbation
is an intrinsically and seriously disordered act . . . the delib-
erate use of the sexual faculty outside normal conjugal relations essentially contradicts the finality of the faculty." The
Sacred Congregation for the Doctrine of the Faith was then
directed by Cardinal Joseph Ratzinger, now known as Pope
Benedict XVI. It is on the same theological basis that the

church continues to denounce homosexuality and indeed any sexual activity not directed toward "the finality": the only and necessary goal of our reproductive capacities. Certain liberal prelates have argued for limited exceptions for masturbatory and other non-procreative sexual activity so long as it leads to the procreative act. Foreplay is OK if it leads to coitus, but only if it leads to penile penetration of an appropriate female.

The last millennium has produced thousands of theological tracts concerning the preconditions and requirements for moral copulation, most of which can be reduced to the argument that moral sex can take place only within the confines of a devotional commitment to creating life. Anything outside such a sacred commitment constitutes a fundamental character disorder that leaves the fornicator further alienated from divine fulfillment. There may be an internal, quasi-Aristotelian logic to the syllogisms, but they are largely bereft of any current psychological insight, and at the end of the night, they leave the church's agents, its priests, with a theological and moral code no more advanced than the hillbilly fundamentalist preachers spew out every Sunday, proclaiming that the world is six thousand years old.

Fortunately, tens of thousands, and possibly as many as half of the world's 405,000 Catholic priests, have given up on strict celibacy (which forbids masturbation) and have

regular sex with willing adults. In 1994, Cardinal Jose San-
chez, of the Vatican's Congregation for the Clergy, generally
agreed to the accuracy of several studies suggesting that at
most 50 percent of priests practice celibacy. Anecdotal evidence suggests as much. A decade or so ago, Carl, a jour-
nalistic colleague who was openly gay and who had earlier
studied for the priesthood, weighed a return to the cloth
and undertook on-site interviews with a number of monastic
communities. A Dominican brotherhood in the South was
particularly keen on Carl. At a critical moment in their discussions, Carl told them of his homosexual life and made it
clear he had no intention of abandoning sex with men. The
brothers smiled at him, he told me, and asked simply, "So
what's the problem?"

Brother Peter has never been so candid with the members of his order. He supposes they do not know of the
friendships and adventures he has shared with me and others. He does not know whether other Dominicans with
whom he shares prayers and silent meals also have their
own adventures with men, or with women. It would not
bother him if they do, but if so, he doesn't want to know—
not because he doesn't care about their affective lives, but
because he believes sharing such intimate knowledge would
threaten the security of the monastic family. That "family"
is the rock of his emotional and spiritual stability. Ordinary parish priests cast into the crosscurrents of faith and

displacement find other solutions. Some have discovered in the hierarchical order of the church a salvation from the disorder of desire. Others, like the Irish child abusers, clearly failed to find adequate solace in the Doctrine of the Faith, and the hierarchy provided them neither charity nor counsel. As Marie Keenan put it, they blew up and took their victims with them. A doubtless larger proportion of those dwindling numbers of Euro-Americans who continue to prostrate themselves for the rites of ordination have successfully negotiated a working balance between their biological compulsions and the real communities of faith to which they have given themselves. In France and Italy, there seems to be a ready wink of the eye when the matter of priestly celibacy comes up in conversation. An old friend from Rome once told me, with only limited irony, that priests, like prostitutes, perform a vital role for adolescent males who want to test out their erotic yearnings so they can decide which gender they prefer. But that was Italy.

Those who have taken up monastic orders are surely of a special nature. No longer do incipient gay men need to seek out the cloisters for refuge from a hostile secular world. Indeed the monastic life today seems to most ordinary people far stranger and more exotic than marching publicly through the streets waving a rainbow flag. To take on the robes and the cowls and the vows of poverty, and often silence, of the monastic life speaks of a genuine spiritual sensibility. In a world of unprecedented sexual openness and opportunity, that spiritual journey is no longer free of the challenges and temptations of the flesh. Certainly that is the case with "Brother Peter," who continues to wrestle with the dual dictates of devotion and desire.

CHAPTER TWO

TRANSUBSTANTIATION

*In which Brother Peter agrees to
interrogation and offers praise to the
Sisters of Perpetual Indulgence.*

New Year's Day, 1986. Sylvester, the titan of queer soul,
took over American television's *Tonight Show*, that evening hosted by the comedian Joan Rivers, and sang his gold-
plated anthem, "You Make Me Feel Mighty Real." A few
minutes later on the talk show set, Rivers asked him how his
parents reacted when they found out he was a drag queen.

"I'm not a drag queen," he retorted. "I'm Sylvester."

Thanks to YouTube, anybody, including Brother Peter, can
call Sylvester back from the grave to relive the moment. My
first conversation with Brother Peter, to my surprise, opened

with the case of Sylvester and what it meant to be "mighty real," what the difference was between Peter's reality in clerical robes, in denim, or in biker leather. He told me about the two drag shows he'd gone to the previous week.

"Drag shows?" I said.

"Yes," he answered in the same tone as if he'd gone to Bach's *St. Matthew Passion*. He had known these particular drag artists for at least ten years. One of them—whose nom de guerre is Madame Raymonde, modeled after the famous heart-of-gold prostitute from the 1930s film *Hôtel du Nord*—had made his name singing in a Parisian piano bar where Brother Peter was an intermittent regular. Brother Peter had seen some of Madame Raymonde's sketches online, but he'd never been to a full-fledged drag show.

"Drag? Why drag?" I asked.

"The idea of changing your personal presence completely, the idea of a 'total transportation.'"

Silently I waited for more. But priest that he was, nothing was forthcoming. It was for me to pose the questions, and when I wanted more, to ask for it. Some people would have stopped the dialogue then. Too much work. The game too tedious. Had he averted his eyes as though bored or genuinely closed off, our encounters might have ended, a glance at the watch, a clearing of the throat, and a shrug. But behind the formality of his confessional training, within the priestliness of the moment, I took his silence instead as a signal of reticent frailty, an indication that he would like to speak and speak not as he would in his formal confessions but to someone he hoped was a kindred spirit.

"So do you make a total transformation in all the identities you wear?" I asked.

"I think I do transform myself, but listen well: all that is form, outside of things. It's obvious that when I'm in the monastic robes that haven't been altered since the Middle Ages or when I'm in street clothes that's a 'transformation.' No question. But I've done nothing to my sexual identity. I'm a man and I remain a man, unlike these boys on stage who change completely their gender from masculine to feminine. But even though I can feel people may look at me differently depending on whether I'm in my monastic habit or in street clothes, I'm still exactly the same person."

Sooner than I'd anticipated we were cutting directly to questions of spirit, flesh, identity, and the most mystical of moments in Christian mythology, transfiguration: What is the nature of the human body, how does it (how do we) express our essential nature, and in expressing what it is that we are, do we touch, are we guided by the light that is the integral beauty of the soul? Or is it still possible even in this passage of testo and twitter identities to hold on to the notion of integral selves and essential souls? We'll return to much of this in a later conversation addressing the question of the Christian idea of an eternal body (old, worn-out, and flabby like Lazarus or the hunky archangel Michael in our family Bible whose warrior physique was one of my earliest jerk-off images). At the beginning of our talks I was much keener to know of Brother Peter's own personal transformations and how he navigated these several identities so clearly linked to his own dress habits—white hooded robe or leather and denim that hugged his ass tight. Underlying Thomistic theology concerning physical transfiguration would have to wait.

We dwelt instead with Madame Raymonde, otherwise known as Denis D'Arcangelo. "Actors live with permanent transformation, becoming other personalities when they're on stage. Off stage when I knew him, he dressed like any other guy," Brother Peter said. "I never saw him looking like a woman, always just a man." Madame Raymonde is rather more like Dame Edna Everage, the Australian cross-dressing comedian, than a real spikes-and-sequins drag queen. Though Dame Edna became a BBC and later an American television phenomenon of the 1980s—and officially at least was straight—Madame Raymonde is far from straight. Her accordion-playing accompanist sometimes joins her in tap-dancing routines, dressed in flimsy flapper-era outfits at overwhelmingly gay clubs. Together they keep a European touring schedule that would have exhausted Sarah Bernhardt. They are everything that Brother Peter is not: slutty, lower class, peppered with sex and the gutter. "[She] often does songs that are very sad, inspired from the demimonde of working-class bistros, of prostitution, of the women and men who work the streets," he began. As he spoke a softness came to his eyes, the suppleness of sympathy crept across his cheeks, not at all like the paternalistic priest ready to take confession, but more that of a fellow traveler who had had his own experience in the worn pathways that trim the bushes of desire and loss. "She comes out of the same tradition as the dance halls of the 1930s that were loose . . . naughty," he added. He looked across the table where the tape recorder spun and began to hum a tune I didn't know. He had agreed that our conversations should be recorded, but only our conversations. His eyes took on the same light he'd used at the Pierre et Gilles show. Our knees connected.

But we were working.

"Well," he went on, "the performance was even more compelling because the poor boy—the accordionist tap dancer—had fallen and broken his knee that evening or maybe the day before, so he had to perform on crutches with his leg in a cast, which meant they had to change the dance routines. He had to be suffering. That is why it was so impressive. The show was very, very beautiful and very touching."

"Touching?"

The hungry, cruising eyes softened toward empathy. "It made me laugh and cry. I cried because in some of their songs—and I believe that's what interests me in these kinds of shows with men who play women—because they can say things about love, about tenderness, about frailty, about the need to be loved that people often don't appreciate or don't forcefully admit when it comes from a tough, virile man. You know, a woman can speak about feeling fragile, her need to be loved, the wounds of love and life, the search for a great love that so often results in disappointment, and thus she can express something more tender, more subtle than a traditional man [can]."

"Why do you think that is?" I asked.

"Because I think that in our civilization, society says that to be a man you have to be strong, you have to be a seducer, you have to be macho. We give very little attention to expressing feelings among men. That's always seen as a weakness."

"It's the same in the Bible isn't it? The men in the Bible, at least in the Old Testament, are emblems of macho ferocity."

"The men of the Bible are able to express their feelings. They can cry, they can say that they love. Take David. David loved. He said so. He cries for those he loves, his friend Jonathan, his son Absalom when he is murdered. He doesn't hesitate to express his feelings, his suffering, or his pain. In the Bible it's more complicated than you say, more complex."

He paused, waiting for me to say something, but this time I remained silent. The Bible my agnostic father insisted I read as one of the foundations of English poetry was also the Bible of fire and brimstone that battered out the hate and bestiality that echoed up and down the Appalachian hollows of my childhood.

"Well. In any case, the show, I can tell you, it touched me deeply."

Brother Peter's use of the Bible was not always as curt and formulaic as that response, but like many religious men who had come to their religious life late—he was well into his twenties when he took his orders—he was always cautious about revealing any fissures of doubt. He insisted that doubt had never touched him since he gave himself over to the order. My companion, Christophe, who was raised in the church, occasionally listened to parts of our conversations; for him, Brother Peter's words varied little from mainline Catholic dogma.

To many gay priests—not a locution Brother Peter uses; he prefers to say that he is a man who is a priest who has homosexual desire—the conflict between desire and religious stricture is insurmountable, as it was for Rafe. The conflict provokes first a terrible wedge of doubt in the ecclesiastical regime, then it challenges the practice, and finally it weakens the faith. But what I found so compelling in our encounters (because our encounters were often as physically engaged as they were intellectually stimulating) was how they seemed actually to reinforce Peter's faith. Faith, he told me at one point, had enabled him to understand the frailty of desire. *Frailty* is a word that came up often. He believed deeply that at a certain point the pure power of faith would release him from desire. It was as though his transformation from being an ordinary, secular young man raised far from Communion and confession into a man of the cloth had itself opened an extraordinary insight into the perpetual tension between soul and flesh. Touching the cusp of early manhood as a fairly standard heterosexual, including erotic adventures with women, he had not been visited by genuine love until he fell into his first grand passion with a man who happened to be a middle-aged priest (about which we will also return to later). Most of my gay and straight friends were ready to dismiss his account as a classic story of a closeted youth who finally realized who he was sexually.

But no, Brother Peter insisted with some agitation that by the simplest measure he had never had any problems becoming aroused by women, and he had no recollection of locker room or campground attractions to other boys or men. First he had a thoroughly unexpected spiritual experience unrelated to any other personal attachment, which led to his initial religious studies, during which he in turn fell in love with the older priest. As he told the story, it was a triple transformation: from nonbeliever to believer, from secular life to spiritual mission, from personal isolation to love. The switch from hetero desire to homo desire was the least profound of these transformations. His first intense spiritual revelations came not as a flight from forbidden desires (the usual clichéd track that took tormented, young gay men to the cloth); rather, his intensifying devotion led him to pursue the multiple contradictions of being fully human. Meanwhile, though he expressed no interest in living within a fully gay context, progressively he needed to engage deeply with the visible, organized gay world. Drag, transvestism, motorcycle clubs, making pickups in art galleries, admiring the hearty male bodies he found in the steam rooms of the public gyms wherever he was sent to preach: these were and are all doors to that experience.

As were his encounters with a group I would have assumed he would detest for its manifest blasphemy: the Sisters of Perpetual Indulgence.

"Mother Rita," he began with another smile.

"Mother Rita?"

"Mother Rita of Calvary, or 'L'archimere Rita du Calvaire.' That's what they called her in France." Brother Peter came to know Mother Rita when he was visiting France and working in Paris. Mother Rita remains the founder and mother superior at the Paris convent of the International Order of the Sisters of Perpetual Indulgence, founded in 1979 in San Francisco. There are now thirty-one convents of the Sisters in eight countries. Regular fare for a soft news day on television, the Sisters—all militant gay men—appear publicly in nun's garb with starched white head dress, whiteface, and often full beards. Along with San Francisco's Cockettes, they are the true mothers of radical gender-fuck.

For a man who takes the word of the Bible seriously, not least the distinction imposed in the Old Testament on the inviolate distinctions between male and female, it was, to say the least, a stretch to hear Brother Peter describe the Sisters as kindred spirits.

"At the beginning," he admitted, "I was a bit shocked, but when I first met some of the boys myself back at the beginning—and some, you know, are no longer with us for health and other reasons—and I spoke with some of my [gay] friends who were in touch with them, and then when I read their website, two things struck me. First their use of certain religious folkloric effects, like their robes and the white cornets on their heads. That didn't bother me too much. After all, that's just folklore [as was women's traditional headdress in their variations from Brittany to the Alps to the Peloponnesus].

"In Europe, when people saw the nun's outfits and headdresses in the nineteenth century, it was a sign of a caregiver, someone who visited the poor, someone who pricked your conscience, overall a positive image that drew people's attention to the plight of the poor. [The Sisters'] presentation . . . oh, maybe it's a bit silly, maybe even a little extreme . . . "

I broke in: "Well, it's an obvious mockery of Catholicism."

"No," he answered, his voice stern, almost irritated. "Curiously not, and they often said to me, when they undertake a public action and they cross paths with real nuns in their habits, they said it always turns out to be a good day and a good action and everything goes well."

"The real nuns aren't annoyed?"

"I don't know myself how the actual nuns react. On the other hand, to mock the actual religious celebrations inside the church, the Mass, the sacraments, then, yes, I would be very much bothered by that because that is not simply folklore like the habits and traditions that exist on the outside of the sacred [rituals]. To touch the things that are more deeply linked to the faith, that I stay away from. But using a cornet or a nun's costume doesn't bother me." He repeated the point to be clear. "To touch prayer or the ritual celebrations inside the church—I am very bothered by actions that touch on what is most profound in the church."

"But wait." I said, "Isn't that forgetting the origins of the Sisters? They started out in San Francisco as a militant homosexual rights group who argued that nearly all religious institutions, and specifically the Catholic Church, have brought on terrible suffering."

He shook his close-cropped, sandy-haired head. "The ones I know, when they discovered who I was, were astonished to meet a real priest in a gay milieu."

"A real priest?"

"A priest ordained by the Catholic Church and not . . . well, you know that among the Sisters there are some who wear the soutane, though that's not always true anymore. And they were often very interested in having a serious religious and spiritual discussion with a member of the Catholic clergy."

"They were not hostile or suspicious?"

"No, not."

"What kind of religious discussions? What did you talk about?"

"Usually they ask, 'Why are you a priest? Why have you chosen that path? What does it mean?' And I say that one day I had a personal encounter, very real, of the presence of God in my life."

Before I go on, and before many of you as readers roll your eyes with the remembered testimony of Tammy Faye or the perennially priapic Reverend Jimmy Swaggart, I should say I grew up surrounded by grade school classmates in Kentucky, usually adolescent girls experiencing the first premenstrual twitches of puberty. They would come to school recounting how on the previous Sunday they had *been saved by Jesus! Oh yes!* A wave of warmth had swallowed them up while they sat on the hard poplar pews as the Savior had entered their breasts and drawn them, half crawling, half running, forward to the altar where they fell to their trembling knees before the preacher, declaring how Jesus had led them into the light of glory. *I was saved! I was saved!* they had cried. And wept. And wept.

Too often, within a year, if not months, these country girls became pregnant by a more local savior who had taken them to the back of the barn for an even more penetrating embrace with the transcendent. In the United States, declarations about witnessing the presence of God in your life are as common as Rice Krispies and Twitter. No serious presidential candidate since Jimmy Carter, neither Democrat nor Republican, has dared present himself to the public without professing the critical presence of God in his life. But in continental Europe—apart perhaps from Poland—such sacred visitations are not the stuff of common conversation. Indeed, they are as rare as poetry inscribed with the quills of carrier pigeons. For Brother Peter, who was raised in a Mediterranean family with no tradition of religious observation, being struck by the light of God was as arresting an experience as it would have been for my grade school classmates to expound on the Heisenberg principle. All these doubt-refracted filters were present in my mind as I listened to his testimony, the sheets in the bedroom rumpled and my tape disk spinning.

"I found myself in a personal, living, real relationship with God and I went to the limit of what this relation would mean for me, which meant committing myself to a religious engagement and accepting ordination to serve the church, to carry forth the word of the Gospel. But the thing that always interests them [the Sisters of Perpetual Indulgence], which is at the heart of the question when I talk with them, is that I don't defend the institution of the church. The formal structure doesn't interest me; I am there as a witness for God, the God who is love and who cares for and watches over all of us. So, they find out that I think more of what God says than the temporal heritage of the church. We can talk about how the church works, but what has always seemed the most interesting for me—and for them as well—is the authentic spiritual or mystical dimension of that history."

"You mean that aside from gay militancy, you find a mystical, spiritual nature with the Sisters?" I asked, credulous.

"I don't say that I found it. I say that they pose the question and that they are keen to encounter someone who lives it."

"And your encounters have never been hostile?"

"I've never had a hostile reaction."

Our conversations frequently returned to Brother Peter's sympathy, even respect for costume, performance, transvestism, leathermen, and the dodgy exuberance that is at the core of what the gender theorists call *performative* identity—after Michel Foucault, Judith Butler, and perhaps most approachable, Eve Kosofsky Sedgwick. They all, from a distinctly secular perspective, saw the gendered clothes we wear as fashioned from the fabrics of social constraint and possibility. Whatever our genes have given us in the apparent biological form of our flesh, the way we present and clothe that flesh comes as a result of the unfolding human story by which we invent our lives. In the heyday of French critical theory during the 1980s, I found myself deeply moved and motivated by the philosophical elegance and zest of its great master, Michel Foucault, already dead (by AIDS). Foucault's key work—at least from my point of view—was his 1960s study of prisons and penitentiaries, *Discipline and Punish*, which argued that the rise of bourgeois capitalism demanded the creation of a self-policing industrial working class. The unified powers of state and capital won the collective good behavior of the workers by inculcating in them a fearful respect of being continually observed and judged for correct performance: timeliness, family duty, deference to authority. Even more than prisons, the public schools were the great enforcers whose primary mission was not to teach literacy but to discipline the young and thereby police the unruly desires of "the dangerous classes." (For a portrait of just how dangerous those classes appeared to polite urban society, take a look at Patrick Suskind's 1985 best seller, *Perfume*, which perfectly portrays the upper-class fear of what can happen when uncontrolled senses are married to the animal taste for blood.)

Eve Kosofsky Sedgwick, one of the best of the queer theorists, wrote movingly of just how provisional our perceptions of masculinity and femininity are, of the hunger of the flesh for the same and for the other. Little by little, however, I came to find all the derivative graduate school discourses that followed in the wake of Foucault and Sedgwick terribly arid. Hundreds of doctorates earned by the followers of the followers of the followers of Foucault were filling up

English department faculties across America. Their convoluted sentences and impenetrable paragraphs crafted in the form of Immanuel Kant seemed to me like intellectual arthropods supping on the desiccated corpses of forgotten desire. They had neither dared to take on a nun's habit nor screw or be screwed by a happy priest who revered both his leather and his robes. When at last, without searching, I came across such a monk, I realized that as much as I had benefited from the genuine insights of the gender theorists, I was more touched by the wings of myth that were the stuff of my priest's daily routine.

Myth. The word, derived from the Greek *mythos*, set apart insight into the uncertain from the hard facts described by *logos*, the sort of knowledge that could be determined by cold, philosophical reasoning. *Logos* was the realm of the elite rulers and thinkers, *mythos* the belief system on which ordinary folk relied to guide them through the torments of dreams, desire, suffering, and hope. We moderns, descendants of Descartes, Locke, and the triumph of rational doubt that was the Enlightenment, have come to take *myth* as a synonym for false belief. We speak of myths as beliefs that reason cannot sustain, even as we blithely refer to the myth of Sisyphus as the original ancestor to the modern existential crisis. The loss of vital myth, I fear, has produced —and this is where Brother Peter and I most clearly converge—a dreadful loss. To live a life devoid of myth is like crossing a Kansas winter in an Eisenhower jeep. The English writer Jeanette Winterson, whose Dantesque tales cross the boundaries of gender, physics, time, and galactic space, speaks as movingly as anyone on the human necessity for myth. Years ago she told Bill Moyers on his PBS series *Faith & Reason* that while rationality "has freed us from many cruel superstitions, many nameless terrors . . . it's not sufficient. There is a mythic truth, which is an imaginative truth, an emotional truth, a way of understanding the world which is not about the facts and the figures, but which is nevertheless valid." Later, following what she described as an arid literary decade, she spoke to an interviewer for the British daily *The Guardian* about the necessity of guarding—though not obsessing about—the ever-present personal wound "that gives you the strength to go forward." In that act of going forward from the wound, she said, you learn that "there are so many separate selves."

To touch those separate selves on a daily basis, as Brother Peter does, or as the Sisters of Perpetual Indulgence do, or as the Greeks who prostrated themselves at the Apollonian temple at Delphi did 2,500 years ago, is to allow yourself to be sucked up into zones of mythic comprehension of human contradiction where reason alone is no aid. It is to give yourself over to what for lack of a better word is the zone of the soul, even as reason tells you that there is not and will not be any way of confirming that souls exist. If it seems contradictory to speak of the soul without being able to marshal the evidence of its existence, then so it is with the place of myth as well. Christian myth, Buddhist myth, Horace, or Harry Potter. We continue to generate greater and lesser myths because, as Winterson has said, they enable us to confront and ruminate on the fierce emotional and educational confusions of our existence that no amount of learning seems able to tame. They give us, or most of us, rocks of stability in the ongoing flow that is never the same from one second to the next. For my own taste, the all-knowing, all-powerful Christian deity that inhabited Brother Peter one day in his eighteenth year is a hoary old critter. I find him far less compelling than the Olympian panoply that called on the Greeks to choose a personal guide from among them and who then marked the earth with mounds and crevices where that god's force was made manifest to his or her followers. Like Brother Peter, who doesn't restrict the idea of grace to his own god but supposes that all those who track a path of decency toward one another will find habitation in the greater soul called eternity, for me it doesn't matter much which mythic force you embrace. All that matters is that it respects the multiplicities that drive us to become inquiring human beings.

Or in plainer talk: To be alive and alert is to perform in an endless drag show, its artfulness measured by how gracefully we change our outer robes of identity.

Nowhere have I been more taken by the mythic zone than in contemporary Naples, whose sexual subculture I wrote about at length in *A Queer Geography*. The late magnificent actor Marcello Mastroianni said shortly before he died that Naples would always remain his favorite city because more than anywhere else, it had successfully profited from American ingenuity while steadfastly resisting the antiseptic orderliness of America. The most clichéd example of Neapolitan chaos is the traffic light, which is considered advisory at best. Neapolitans don't hesitate to cross into the opposing lane of traffic, even if they're facing an oncoming streetcar, if they feel that fate is with them. The sense of fate, another way of dealing with the unknown, blankets Neapolitans like the dust of Vesuvius, no less in matters of sex than in its half-pagan, half-Christian attitude toward death and the afterlife.

I went there to learn about the city's famous *femmenielli*, a word used to describe those born with male anatomies but who function and dress as females. The *femmenielli*, well known to American sailors stationed at the U.S. naval base outside Naples who have long been their most reliable clients, are not to be confused with the more modern idea of being "gay." For the most part they have been raised in working-class families—often in the rough Quartieri Spagnoli—who early on perceived that their little boys, sometimes as young as three or four, were not simply boys. One of the *femmenielli* I spoke to carried a full set of male equipment but had been raised in girls' dresses by her parents and married off at age fifteen to a rugged fisherman who was completely straight. They'd been "married" by a local priest and appeared to be perfectly comfortable—after more than twenty years of "marriage." Other *femmenielli* I met worked the streets by night servicing sailors both as tops and bottoms; then by day they worked as babysitters for their neighbors who were off at work and who regarded them as both exceptionally sensitive and superbly reliable.

For the rest of the Neapolitans, however, the *femmenielli* were better known as interpreters of mystical, and mythic, signs. Each night on local television, the number of the following day—a kind of lotto for what to expect— would be chosen from a machine of bouncing, colored, and numbered ping-pong balls. The *femmenielli*, always as buxom and beautifully coiffed as movie stars, would interpret that number as it related to viewers' birthdays, saints days, and other life indicators.

Why, I asked a local friend, Claudio, who knew many *femmenielli*, were they the ones chosen to draw the numbers on TV? "Because," he said, "people, they know, at least they believe, that *femmenielli* have a kind of special vision. Because you know they are both man and woman and, well, not really man or woman, we think, people think, they can see things that we cannot see. They can see who we are, and maybe they see better than us the future." Claudio paused. "Maybe," he said, and smiled.

A decade later I belatedly came across the work of the French social philosopher Michel Maffesoli, a man whose one-time defense of a doctoral study of astrology and science rained a barrage of criticism from more conventional social scientists. Maffesoli, a great admirer of the German social philosopher Georg Simmel, has long been fascinated by what he calls "the feminine or homosexual shadow part" of what are generally regarded as the humdrum activities of contemporary life—from show business to architectural design to the conduct of law and politics. We cannot drive down any of the world's great cosmopolitan boulevards without being reminded—on billboards, by the drivers of buses, by the shape of the shoes of oncoming pedestrians, by the dissolving differences between purses and briefcases— that identities of male and female grow more fluid by the month. Only among the Taliban is identity still presumably fixed, and it's not sure even there, given the reports of Taliban warlords shooting it out for control of each other's alleged boy lovers.

The ubiquity of contradictory androgyny in the public market zone has become linked to the breakdown of gendered household life in Maffesoli's universe, and that linkage has in turn returned us to a renewed hunger for the presence of the mythic, for a set of stories in which we can feel at home. We see and silently accept a version of ourselves that at once contradicts how we comport ourselves publicly in daily life because survival in the modern world requires us to unite with that which is our utter opposite (or our many opposites). This so-called organicity (or *coïncidentia oppositorum*, in the language of Medieval alchemists) was once attributed to the Gaia figure of the all-embracing female life force. Maffesoli says we modern humans feel more and more compelled to test the limits of our inside-out identities, to wear our otherness as easily as we mix *hot* underwear with frumpy hunting jackets. We make of ourselves and our communities a fertile union of androgynous necessity. It takes but the breeziest Google search to find the antecedents to all this in Nordic shape-shifters like Loki, who was variously a salmon, a man, a woman, and a mare; or nearly all the Greek pantheon, perhaps most terrifyingly when Circe turns Ulysses's sailors into swine; or the fearsome vampires born in Transylvania and transported under the pen of Anne Rice to the Garden District of New Orleans. Despite the commandments of the three great monotheistic deities, fluid and multiple identities are more with us than ever.

Maffesoli, a more or less Marxist postmodernist social anthropologist, presses his argument further. As much as we may need myth personally to help us touch that which we cannot fully know, we also rely on myth collectively to shepherd us through the chaos of the larger world. The same Al-Qaeda warlords that fight over Afghan boys don't hesitate to toss rival homosexuals from the tops of five-story buildings, especially when they question core myths about Mohammed. Devout Calvinist ministers keep regular company with multiple extracurricular mistresses. Crusading financial reformers sequester rainy-day margin accounts in offshore fiscal paradises. Any and all are easily dismissed as simple hypocrites, as they have been for centuries, but when the myths they have helped foster are also placed in collective jeopardy, and when the ubiquitous digital media render their flaws instantly accessible to millions in a half dozen key strokes, the threat of social and psychological chaos grows exponentially. For Maffesoli the disjunctive terrain of modern life leaves us unable to escape the digital plenitude of otherness, and it is thus through the zone of myth we might be able to establish a "chain of union," a territory beyond our individual, momentary material necessity where we can recover the quietness and modesty to recognize that all those global antagonists that pepper the internet exist not only in other worlds but also fully within ourselves and our own uncertain identities. The reality of fungible identity more than ever calls us to the territory of myth, be it geographical, spiritual, political, or even sexual.

Of course, Brother Peter, who roots his thinking in the work of the great Dominican theologian Thomas Aquinas, never characterized his embrace of the Christian myth in quite that way. His mythos is the mystery of the Trinity and the magic by which the Holy Spirit manifested itself as a physical, corporal body, thereby showing the way for all humans to find in their personal identities a route to universal transcendence.

Refreshingly, and much to my initial surprise, his eschatology still leaves plenty of space for other non-Christian roads to spiritual and material reconciliation—be they Norwegian shape-shifter stories or Neapolitan *femmenielli*. The mission is to continue the search for understanding, knowing that what is real can never be fully known but only sensed. Our duty is to help each other out along the way, or as the late sequined Sylvester sang, to do whatever we can to make those we care about "feel mighty real."

CHAPTER THREE

The Perils of Porn

*In which Brother Peter leads our
inquisitor into the perils and pleasures
of pornography and the folkloric
history of masturbation.*

If, reader, it isn't already obvious, let me be clear: sex is not a theoretical appetite for Brother Peter. He likes penetration—forward and backward. Always with protection, unless the penetrating object is inanimate. He expressed no sense of shame or anguish about making sex. He is an altogether normal male. Neither is he an adherent to "liberation theology." He is utterly clear that priests, and especially monks living in religious communities, cannot, indeed must not, engage in committed sexual, loving relationships, either of the homo or the hetero variety. Yet unlike Saint Augustine, the fifth-century rake whose later philosophical and theological writing condemned all "concupiscent desire" and nonprocreative "venereal acts," Brother Peter finds penetrative sex a genuine human value. However, were he to say so publicly, he would certainly risk being defrocked, and as a member of the clergy he could even be excommunicated.

Several weeks after our first exchange, on another sunny, brisk day, Brother Peter again passed through Paris with a planned stop by my place after lunch. It was too cold to sit on the terrace, so we lingered for only a few minutes, leaning on the railing beside a planter of early tulips. From that spot, if you look to the right, you get possibly the best view in Paris of the dome of the Panthéon; at night the great spotlight atop the Eiffel Tower scans the rooftops. To counter the chill I began giving Peter a vigorous back and neck massage. Nordics more than any other males I've known readily succumb to deep massage, as did he until I touched a spot just to the right of his left scapula, provoking a more than minor whimper.

He flinched sharply, bunching his shoulders in pain.

"Sorry," I said.

"An injury from a long time ago."

"Yes."

"Not important."

"You jumped like it was important."

"Umm." Then he turned toward me, his back to the rail. "Crazy thing. When I was in the army—"

"Wait, wait," I cut him off. "A military wound? In which war?"

He laughed. "A football injury [meaning soccer]. We were playing football and three guys collided at full speed on top of me while I was guarding the goal."

"That sounds hot. Three soccer jocks in their khaki shorts piled on top of you."

He pinched my nose. "Not at all. They all got up. I just lay there unable to move. Neither my legs nor my arms. I was afraid they'd broken my back. They carried me off the field on a hard stretcher and operated that night."

"I didn't see any scar the last time you came over."

"When the soul is pure, the flesh is restored," he said.

"And both of yours are pure?"

"You can look."

I pushed up his jersey. Though the scar was faint, the fine track of the surgeon's knife paralleled his spine. He shivered in the breeze and pulled down his shirt.

"Right, it's time to put aside play and get to work, but maybe the scarred body is a good place to start."

"I thought the subject was masturbation," he answered with a twinkle.

"OK. Masturbation it is. We can return to the stigmata of the eternal flesh later."

Conversations with Brother Peter always bounce about with an uncertain coherence from one subject to the next, but masturbation—if by that we can assume self-stimulation aided either by another person or by erotic images—was never far away. Aside from my straight Jesuit-educated friend who had never masturbated before losing his virginity, I've never known any males who had not engaged in the so-called secret sin, usually starting no later than age fourteen. Brother Peter was no exception. He'd been jacking off since the first adolescent night he'd learned how. What did surprise me was his expansive knowledge of gay porn, gained mostly from DVDs but also from the seedy sex-movie houses that are often clustered around the world's major train stations.

"Porn houses are important in your life?" I asked him provocatively. When I listened to the recording of our conversation some months later, my voice registered shock, while his response seemed to suggest he thought it a dumb question.

"Not having any other way to live my sexuality, I go there to dream about the things I can never do."

"But you do do those things."

"Yes and no."

"I think I'd say yes," I countered, referring plainly to our earlier romps.

"Look, if you live in a small town, you're known for what you do. More than in cities, what you do defines who you are. You take a big risk by that sort of activity, of being found out, of being denounced, of being attacked, of I don't know what. You don't have complete freedom to do what you want when you're known for who you are."

Often we seemed to circle around and around the subject, but what I most wanted to understand was how Brother Peter regarded fundamental church teaching that has existed for a thousand years apparently forbidding any sexual orgasm not intended for procreation. I well understood that even under the ultraconservative Irish brand of Catholicism, parish priests mostly ignored the formal teaching on masturbation. Once during the height of the AIDS epidemic I heard the pastor of San Francisco's Most Holy Redeemer Church, in the gay Castro District, deliver a homily about the duty to take care of one another. He clearly did not follow the strict Vatican line and even made a fairly loose remark declaring that no one in the Castro was truly "anti-body." As intended, the line drew lots of guffaws. Yet a believer's perception of the body, of the body's potential for generating pleasure, cuts to the very core of Catholic faith. As a man who celebrated both his body and the sacred body, Brother Peter had constructed a finely rendered façade on the subject, and I needed to break past it.

On the table between us, where my companion and I had had breakfast a few hours earlier, lay a copy of *Têtu*, the French gay monthly that always features prime beefcake.

The lad in this issue was a little duskier than usual, a

trimmed pubic chorus plainly visible above his skimpy and tumescently inscribed underwear.

"How about that guy?" I asked pushing the glossy magazine across the table. "Do you find him hot?"

Brother Peter studied the photo and flipped through a few more pages to examine the standard beach spread and another with the stud boy reclined on a weight lifter's bench. Then he closed the magazine.

"I don't know. I would have a different opinion on what makes a handsome guy. The [porn] actors work out a lot, but their bodies are not natural. They've been worked up, almost manufactured according to certain ideals of masculinity, intended to exalt a kind of exaggerated virility. They have to have thick, defined biceps, their abs hard and creased. They're caricatures. They have to spend hours in the gym. And after all that, their faces might or might not express anything interesting."

"But you told me there are truly good porn actors. What makes a good porn actor? What do you look for to get off?"

"Somebody who's convincing, who expresses sensuality in what he's doing. A lot of them show nothing. They feel nothing. They're mechanical, while others use their bodies and gestures to reveal intense sensuality. They are happy and show it in what they're living and doing, and that happiness shows. They're convincing, like an actor in the theatre who makes us believe in his character. Otherwise, he's a bad actor."

Brother Peter's dialogues about sex and the body always advanced on two levels. On the surface they were fairly obvious, almost banal. Who doesn't prefer to watch people making love who seem to be really passionate with each other, physically as well as emotionally? At the same time, Brother Peter's responses were deeply shaped by his religious education even if not always consciously so. He knew well the church's most important thinkers, from Saint Augustine to Karl Barth and Teilhard de Chardin. He had read most of them in their original languages—Greek, Latin, French, Provençal, Spanish, or German. (Did I fail to say he was a master linguist?). Most important to him, however, were Thomas Aquinas and Saint Augustine, whom I had read only lightly and even so more than thirty years earlier in a sophomore humanities class. To talk seriously about faith and masturbation, I was constrained to do some homework.

For both Aquinas and Augustine, the sexual use of the human body was a core concern. From early adolescence on, Augustine had ravaged every attractive (presumably female) person he could lure into a barn or a back alley in the Roman outpost of Hippo (now Annaba in Algeria) before he turned fiercely celibate. Thomas Aquinas, the first great Dominican theologian, sought to rationalize Augustine's later essays on the body with Aristotelian reason. No territory is omitted in the Thomistic meditations. Lust, fornication, masturbation, even nocturnal emissions rise to scrutiny.

Permit me a brief theological digression before we return to the act itself. It begins with, in Augustinian Latin, the question of whether *actus venerus*, or sexual acts, can ever be without sin. Augustine, having engaged in apparently thousands of them, said no, no matter where, no matter with whom, no matter how.

As severe as the repentant Augustine was in his judgment of "venereal acts," Aquinas was balanced and deliberative. Augustine saw sex as in itself sinful regardless of its circumstance, a consequence of Adam and Eve's fall from grace. Thus, even though sexual procreation was evidently necessary for the survival of the species, all humans are inevitably born in and of sin, or in Augustine's own words, "I consider that nothing so casts down the manly mind from its height as the fondling of a woman, and those bodily contacts." As a result, the highest and most sacred behavior humans could engage in was to renounce the corrupting appetites of the flesh through prayer and contemplation of God. Given that desire is an integral element of the body, therefore, the human body on this earth is itself "corrupt" or "impure."

Now Brother Peter—as opposed to Peter the man of flesh—had become genuinely Augustinian. He longed to be free of his "corrupt appetites." He longed for a penis that always slept, a prostate that was forever contrite. Following his theological education, he felt his flesh as an imprisoning cage. And yet, the tensions and dimensions of the physical cage that defined Peter the man had, he told me, intensified Brother Peter's spiritual quest, leading him to a greater understanding of the physical and emotional complexities of other men. (His comprehension of women and the female dynamic of liberation and capture, it's fair to say, was more limited.) Not that he entered into Augustinian meditation inside all the sleazy porn houses he visited or that he blathered into Thomistic logic during ecstatic penetration (as one Navy SEAL I once encountered had done.) Peter's physiological functions were fully of the physical moment. On these occasions he was always simply Peter the middle-aged male. All the same, Peter the man was regularly in dialogue with Brother Peter the monk, and I have to admit that that dialogue intensified the richness and the excitement of our periodic encounters.

Of course, having fallen into the arms of the Dominicans, Brother Peter had grown closer to Thomistic logic than to Augustinian darkness, just as Aquinas himself had employed Aristotelian logic to engage with Augustine: All virtue, Aquinas argued, must be based on "right reason," for right reason is that knowledge imparted explicitly by the all-knowing God. How, then, are we to make sense of the desiring, sexual body created by this same God? First Aquinas asserts that "no sin is committed in that which is against neither nature, nor morals, nor a commandment."

Following that basic principle, he goes on:

> A sin, in human acts, is that which is against the order
> of reason. Now the order of reason consists in its order-
> ing everything to its end in a fitting manner. Where-
> fore it is no sin if one, by the dictate of reason, makes
> use of certain things in a fitting manner and order for
> the end to which they are adapted, provided this end
> be something truly good. Now just as the preservation
> of the bodily nature of one individual is a true good,
> so, too, is the preservation of the nature of the human
> species a very great good. And just as the use of food
> is directed to the preservation of life in the individual,
> so is the use of venereal acts directed to the preserva-
> tion of the whole human race. Hence Augustine says
> (De Bono Conjug. xvi): "What food is to a man's well
> being, such is sexual intercourse to the welfare of the
> whole human race." Wherefore just as the use of food
> can be without sin, if it be taken in due manner and
> order, as required for the welfare of the body, so also
> the use of venereal acts can be without sin, provided
> they be performed in due manner and order, in keeping
> with the end of human procreation.

The preservation of humanity follows, by elemental logic,
the dictates of right reason; therefore it is a good—a position

easily endorsed and cited by the Vatican's most conservative theologians still today. But, of course, the sex that I and others have with Brother Peter is not in the least concerned with procreation, nor will it be in the foreseeable future. Yet traditional Catholic theology has been rather picky about which elements of Aquinas it chooses to embrace. For in his third sentence Aquinas also said that there "is no sin if one, by the dictate of reason, makes use of certain things in a fitting manner and for the end to which they are adapted, provided this end be something *truly good* [emphasis mine]."

Here a growing body of science, not to mention gay rights advocacy, comes into conflict with both Aquinas and Vatican instruction. While Aquinas and Augustine both reject nonmarital intercourse and the penetration of man by man as against the rule of nature, and therefore a corruption of "right reason," contemporary naturalist observation leaves no doubt that the theologians were dead wrong. Nearly all birds and animals regularly copulate with partners that are not their mates, and for at least the female's interest, they do so to further enrich the complexity of DNA and the hardiness of the species. Fluffing about outside the nest turns out to be a fundamental evolutionary value for ensuring the sturdiness of those born inside the nest. A parallel value appears to be true for mammalian homosexuality, as Bruce Bagemihl demonstrated exhaustively in *Biological Exuberance: Animal Sexuality and Natural Diversity.* Why more or less all species want, and apparently need, to express some homosexual desire remains an unanswered question. But that it is a natural desire is no longer contestable.[1]

Even more pointedly, same-sexers—to use the late Gore Vidal's preferred term—appear in large proportion to have an integral and *natural* need to find psychic and spiritual fulfillment through same-sex coitus. We need to fondle, caress, and penetrate our own. As for the matter of male orgasm itself, all doubt has also disappeared concerning its value to the healthy prostate. My personal doctor in Paris, who used to have her own televised sexual advice program, recommends at least four orgasms per week for young and middle-aged males as a measure to prevent prostate disease or cancer later in life. A U.S. National Cancer Institute study of thirty thousand men, as well as a parallel Australian study, also found measurably lower incidence of prostate cancer in men who ejaculate several times per week. Repeated prostate stimulation and ejaculation are clearly built into the natural function of the human male, irrespective of his need or interest in procreation.

Were a philosopher of Aquinas's reason and balance alive today and served the evidence that is now available, it certainly is arguable that his critique of Augustine would have been even harsher than it was in the thirteenth century. For those of us who do pass a third of our hours on the mattress with others of our own sex, our drives appear not only not at variance with nature in general but also contributive to "a very great good" and therefore consistent with the principle of "right reason." Aquinas's argument against nonprocreative lustful activities must, therefore, be judged not by what Brother Peter calls "folkloric" religious practice but by how these activities enrich human bonding and the comprehension of other souls. All recorded time and geography have held well documented places both for those whose physical presentation contradicts heterosexual convention and whose erotic life is unconcerned with propagation, which leads us back to masturbation and the healthy, or unhealthy, uses of porn in Brother Peter's life.

"Isn't it true," I asked him, "that celibacy forbids the priest or the monk even from touching himself sexually, from masturbating, indeed from enjoying orgasm at all?" He nodded in agreement, adding that some of the rules enforced on young seminarians in the 1950s were so bizarre as to be hallucinogenic. "Some of the seminarians could not even look at themselves naked in the mirror; their bodies always had to be covered. At one point in the seminaries you couldn't even tuck your shirt into your pants with your hands because your hand could not touch your sex. It could go that far. I've spoken with older priests who were trained in the '50s, and it's true that there was in effect an inability to talk in emotional, affective, or sexual terms. That's how the rule of celibacy was understood."

"But that amounts to a denial of your own body," I said, "of your own physicality."

"Yes. Totally. I think that the emotional or affective development of certain generations of priests was damaged. It's true. Still, a lot of things have changed today. Having worked with the training of religious youth myself I can say that [religious education now] is much broader and takes into account much more the range of the personality of the young, including their emotional lives, the place of friendship and love in their existence, and at the same time [tries] to understand what the call to celibacy truly is about."

"The call to celibacy?" I'd never heard it expressed quite like that.

Peter set aside the issue of *Têtu* that he'd been casually thumbing and looked at me more intently. "The reason one chooses not to be married is not a refusal of something that is bad in itself. It's a question of seeing something greater, something positive and not simply because the church demands it." He paused. "There have been many different practices in the history of the church. In the early days, it's clear that the bishops were called to celibacy."

"When?"

"The third or fourth century. And if they were married at the moment they were called, they had to separate from their wives or promise to live like brother and sister. That was obviously difficult, so they preferred that their wives go away and live in religious communities when it was possible. Starting in the fourth century in the Western, Latin Church, they began to argue for celibacy for priests and also for the lay deacons, while the Eastern [Orthodox] Church agreed to ordain men who were already married and permitted them to live with their wives." The same remains true today.

Again, we were circling and circling, as is so often the case in intellectual Catholicism, where in the tradition of Thomas Aquinas, truth is to be found in the finest distinctions of tradition and behavior. The more we conversed, the more I came to understand how deeply Brother Peter was moved by the arguments and conflicts among the church's founding thinkers, most of whom lived well before the Renaissance. Yet before me also sat a man of this century, a patron of video porn that he judged not—apparently— according to theological citations but by how convincing the performers were on camera as sexual animals, and moreover sexual human animals who could bring him to the absolutely impure act of masturbatory orgasm.

"If you look back at the penitents, as we call them in church history, when they created the catalogue of faults and sins for which you have to do penance, until the twelfth century, masturbation had not appeared. It was hardly spoken of. It wasn't a problem."

"Surely," I broke in, "it's obvious to anyone who observes that dogs and most other animals engage in some sort of masturbation."

"No," he continued, "that's not the point. The entire

problem revolves around taboos and ritual purity, which comes from the Old Testament, and continued to occupy the universe of man in the Middle Ages. If you had a nocturnal emission, even if it was completely involuntary, you were impure and you could not celebrate Mass. Even if it was unconscious! It's the idea of taboo and impurity—versus the concept of sin. The idea that masturbation was a sin came much later, inspired by the Gospels and rediscovered in the philosophical works of Aristotle and the Stoics who could only engage in 'fertile' sexual acts intended for reproduction. Even in these pagan systems, the sex act was only accepted from the point of view of fertility. Thus, 'solitary sex' or homosexual sex were necessarily excluded because they couldn't be fertile. It was only in the thirteenth century that the church returned to this discourse and borrowed heavily from the ancients.

"In the Gospels, Jesus was not so clear. In the Old Testament there was one man who gave his name to solitary sex. Onan, of onanism. He was condemned in the Bible not because he masturbated [but] because he was supposed to take his dead brother's wife. Biblical law said that if a man dies without issue, the brother must take his widow to create a posterity for him, which means he must have children with the widow, and those children will be looked on as the children of the dead brother. Onan didn't want to give children to his dead brother. He wanted children of his own, so he declined to fertilize [his sister-in-law]."

"Now wait, Peter [I couldn't bring myself to call him Brother Peter, regardless of our sex roles], that's not exclusively Christian. You find the same cultural rules throughout the tribes of North Africa and the Middle East—now as then."

"Exactly!" he exclaimed. "But these sorts of ideas spread across the West. The worst enemies of masturbation were not restricted to the Catholic clergy but to a certain number of physiocrats during the eighteenth and nineteenth centuries who were obsessed by male masturbation: the loss of energy, the loss of the seed, not creating children—and not at all for religious reasons. It was all about economics and society."

"So, what you're saying is that when you jack off to images of hairy hunks screwing each other in porno films, the so-called sin comes not from the Bible and Jesus's teaching, but from secular, or as you say, 'folkloric' tradition?"

"Absolutely. It's a question of fertility and of replacing [a nation's] population. That's why men should not spill their seed. That campaign was launched by the physiocrats."

Another brief digression. Let me confess: I had never heard of the physiocrats, nor had any of my friends aside from one who is a specialist in eighteenth-century philosophy. Preachments against the "secret sin" as I'd always understood them were just that: "preaching" by the sober elders of the churches, most of them black-robed Catholics. Could it be true that the church was a little tagalong to a nationalist, socioeconomic movement more or less allied with the birth of capitalism? A quick set of phone calls to a few historians and even a cursory internet search of the documents seem to confirm Brother Peter's explanation.

Though all but unknown today to American university students, the physiocrats were one of the bizarre confections of early British capitalism and the French Enlightenment. Roughly coterminous with Adam Smith, the intellectual founding father of market economics, a Franco-Swiss physician, Samuel Auguste David Tissot, produced a screed published in 1760 titled *L'Onanisme*, which argued that the vile practice was the cause of most of those dreadful maladies we were still being warned about in the 1960s, among them blindness, deafness, rickets, even tuberculosis. Still earlier, in 1712, the English quack John Marten had published *Onania, or, The Heinous Sin of Self Pollution and all its Frightful Consequences, in both SEXES Considered, with Spiritual and Physical Advice to those who have already injured themselves by this abominable practice. And seasonable Admonition to the Youth of the nation of Both SEXES.* At the core of the physiocratic dogma was the conviction that workers both in the field and in the factory must be disciplined to provide the labor necessary for a vigorous and altogether secular economy—an ethic that could not tolerate the notion that free individuals could tend to their own private pleasures.

Brother Peter's protest against blaming the Catholic Church for the campaigns against masturbation (and *pari passu* his apologia for finding his own release through the finer arts of DVD porn) not only surprised me but also sent me to look further into the sources of the campaign. If the Enlightenment physiocrats and the free-market capitalists had fired passions in Europe against solitary pleasures, the campaign against jerking off across the Atlantic took on a peculiarly American color.

Tissot's book condemning onanism didn't reach America until 1832, but it quickly became a text for a growing army of antiphysicalists, a movement that was allied at times with the abolitionists, the Temperance movement, and even some sectors of early feminism. One Sylvester Graham published *A Lecture to Young Men on Chastity* about the same time as the new "male purity" movement began. A slew of "doctors" and self-styled mental health experts rapidly joined the ranks, arguing that masturbation was a cause of insanity. Cultural historian Michael Moon cites the "case" of a so-called reformed masturbator recorded in the *Lecture*: "[He] commenced the practice very young; and before he was aware of its ruinous effects, he had nearly destroyed his constitution . . . [He] was never able so completely to overcome the effects of his former error, as to give his system that constitutional vigor, and power of endurance and resistance, which belong to those who have never greatly violated the laws of nature."

But why at just that moment, when the rigid Puritan grip on American life had all but dissolved and the nation was possibly at the apogee of anticlerical sentiment?

Though American communities arguably were more deeply entwined with their churches than either their French or English counterparts, still the campaign did not arise directly from the pulpits. It came at two levels: one ideological and the other from the desperate hunger for population as America expanded economically and geographically.

Throughout the first decades of the nineteenth century, Americans were largely small-town people whose lives revolved around farming and the physical trades—carpentry, masonry, blacksmithing. As they moved westward they created more and more utopian communities made famous by the writers Hawthorne, Thoreau, Emerson, and Robert Owen. Various forms of free love and even the sort of comradely physical affection later celebrated in the Calamus poems of Walt Whitman's *Leaves of Grass* drew a wide following. They took the original Puritan settlers' notions of America as a vision for remaking the world and reimagined it as socialist-voluntarist utopia that celebrated human bodies and souls free of Protestant damnation. Little surprise that traditionalists, whether or not they still felt allied to the churches, would strike back, and so they did through the purity movements, the jeremiads against evil drink, and the creation of the sort of penitentiaries (places where offenders should become penitent) that Michel Foucault dissected in *Discipline and Punish*. A full-fledged war broke out over the right of human beings to own and control their bodies. Chastity and antimasturbation became battle cries for the conservative traditionalists.

Equally, the repressive campaigns coincided with the two most profound social forces in the growth of the nation: "winning of the West" and the consequent desperate need for immigrants to populate that frontier. As profoundly as the Israelites and the other tribes of the Biblical era required an expanding population, so did America. They came, as we all know, by the hundreds of millions from all over the world bearing their own moral codes and languages. Being immigrants, they were also cut off from their old heritages. Freed from the constraints of family decorum, they were by all reports uncommonly lusty. Whether in New York's infamous Five Points or on the Chicago River waterfront or in the stews along the banks of the Schuylkill in Philadelphia, men and women, though poor, were romping with unprecedented physical exuberance. If the upper-class intellectuals envisioned pastoral free-love utopian towns, the mass of Irish, German, Slavic, and later Italian immigrants were screwing and masturbating (and raping) all over the back alleys and sometimes the boulevards of the exploding cities. Crime—murder, robbery, gang vendettas—ran rampant and indeed threatened the sobriety and reliability of the workforce on which the new industrial nation most depended. A free body was the enemy of a disciplined workforce, and the first step toward suppressing the idea of a free body was to suppress the first temptation of adolescent boys from pleasuring themselves alone or in groups. As Thomas Laqueur, the master historian of masturbation, has recounted in exquisite detail (*Solitary Sex: A Cultural History of Masturbation*), the suppression of solitary sex in America, and in Europe, was far more a socioeconomic phenomenon than a simple consequence of Puritan or Catholic hysteria.

None of that history, of course, ought to absolve today's arid medieval minds who continue to fuel contemporary Vatican pronouncements about the evil of nonprocreative sex and the profound moral stain that drenches Catholic doctrine on the matter of condoms for the prevention of AIDS and myriad other diseases. For his own part as a faithful soldier of the church, Brother Peter steadfastly refuses to attack the hierarchy no matter how much his own behavior departs from doctrine, be it about masturbation or cocksucking. Nor ought we forget that the official church lends no quarter to magazines like *Têtu* or DVD porn or any of the midnight gay porn movies widely available on European cable television channels.

"So," I asked after Brother Peter's seminar had concluded, "buying and using gay porn doesn't pose a problem for you as a priest or as a monk?"

How silly of me to have expected a simple response. His answers were never simple. "It's true that I watch porno movies, but at the same time I always have . . ." He sighed. He shifted about at the table and looked at me with sadness. "I see these boys on the screen and sometimes I find out things about their lives from the papers and it turns out they are seropositive. They are on drugs . . . they've died from overdoses. They've committed suicide; they've failed to build a real life. That poses a huge question for me. [I don't feel bad or guilty] for my own dreams and fantasies, but I have to ask myself, How did that happen? What pushed them into that life? What unhappiness was behind it all? What did they have aside from being regarded by others as pure sex fantasies?"

"Sure, that's a fair question and a real moral concern," I answered, "but depression and drug overdoses and suicides plague all kinds of work. In the U.S. and parts of Europe, farmers lead the list of suicides and doctors are among the leading IV drug users."

He wrinkled his nose and eyebrows with a measure of exasperation. "The problem, you know as well as I, is that pornography [is erected on] a slippery slope. You can lose yourself very fast. Look at the gay porno industry. There are more and more bareback films where guys are swallowing cum. That raises troubling problems about what kind of 'gift' porn films make. Is that acceptable? Come with me to Berlin or even here in Paris. I can take you to a place that specializes in them, one whole shelf. You'll see. You can watch them on the videos in the bars."

"What do you think that's about?"

"It's nothing new. It's been going on for some time. People are fed up with AIDS and putting limits on their pleasure. There are also sadistic scenes that go too far."

I was preparing to suggest that there is far more real sadism in straight porn marketed to chain hotels all over the world, not to mention home videos made by American soldiers raping and torturing their prisoners at Abu Ghraib, but our conversation had reached its end. He looked at his watch and began to fidget. The day had grown long. He had an old friend, also gay but not a Christian, who was in need of counseling and a responsive ear. Indeed his many gay friends scattered across several cities were often, he said, not practicing Christians. That posed no problem for him. The cloth was the cloth. Jeans were jeans. While his sentiments about the notion of mutual giving and mutual sacrifice derived from his faith, they were never limited to those within that faith. The conversation had been stimulating, he assured me, but we would have to take up masturbation on another visit.

"After you've confessed your impurities?" I said, giving him a gentle tummy poke.

He smiled, slipped on a sweatshirt, pulled up the hood to protect his shiny head, and gave me a gentle peck on either cheek.

ENDNOTE:

1. The last thirty years have seen a rich dialogue initiated by E. O. Wilson, the Harvard evolutionary biologist who in 1975 attempted to draw a parallel between humans and certain highly organized insects, including ants, where homosexual behavior appears present in group behavior. Posing the possibility of a gene or set of genes that might extend a "eusocial" value to homosexuality, he posed a situation in which two groups are engaged in fierce competition, one exclusively heterosexual and the other inclusive of homosexual members who functioned as "'helpers' in hunting or child rearing: they bore no children but they helped kin to raise their close genetic relatives. If groups with homosexual helpers prevailed in competition over exclusively heterosexual groups, then homosexuality genes would have been maintained by kin selection." A number of Wilson's friends and colleagues were quick to acknowledge the logic of Wilson's position, but they also pointed out the absence of any genetic research to confirm it. More recently Wilson suggested a more tempered version to explain the ubiquity of homosexuality in insects and mammalian groups and wondered whether the behavior "may give advantages to the group by special talents, unusual qualities of personality, and the specialized roles and professions it generates." While sociobiologists are yet to demonstrate any clear utility for homosexuality in either kinship or nonkinship groups, what has become clear along the way is that the behavior is nearly universal among highly organized species, that it presents no negative social consequence to those groups, and that nothing in "nature"—as Aquinas and the Vatican would have it—links homosexual activity with evolutionary decline or degradation.

CHAPTER FOUR

THE FUNCTION OF FORNICATION

In which Brother Peter contemplates
the biological nature of fornication
in the light of Augustine, Thomas
Aquinas, and Aristotle.

Another month passed before Brother Peter was back in town, and as usual we arranged our encounter just after lunch. As far as I could tell, his idea of lunch was little more than a cup of yoghurt. The coffee and the extras were my responsibility.

"So how many Hail Marys since last month?" I asked after the preliminaries were concluded.

"Are you asking for more punishment?" he responded with a less than angelic regard.

"That's not really a direct answer."

"What's the question?"

"Sex. It's still not clear to me about how you reconcile having sex either alone or with another man and your vow of celibacy. For Saint Augustine all sex was sticky with sin. For you, a Catholic priest, to admit having sex is to admit to overt sin."

"I didn't *admit* it. I told you. *Admit* sounds like I'm ashamed. I'm not at all."

"OK, but is sex a sin for you?"

"Sexuality in itself is not a sin. It's a normal part of human biology. I have the same hormonal, genital, and reproductive system as anyone and it functions like any other man's. For me *sin* poses a question of what you do, how you live, and how you use sex. Is it an outlet that permits you to express love with someone, or is it only a conquest? A search for pleasure? Is it a way to give something to another person and be able to hear the other, to be attentive to another, or is it only using others for yourself? That is the question for me."

Was I hearing a devout Dominican monk, or was it Alan Watts reincarnated or Meher Baba? These lines bore little resemblance to the arguments made by Dominican founder Thomas Aquinas much less to Pope Benedict XVI. However, to be polite and to encourage Brother Peter on, I bit my doubts.

"The same thing goes with many married couples, men

and women preparing for marriage and living together afterward. I've seen many who've had to work to figure out how to manage sex between themselves. The rhythm of desire is often not at all the same or expressed in the same way, or they don't know how to be patient in the same way. The man has to pay attention to being reciprocal to his wife. He has to accept that a woman is not just an available sex object whenever and however he wants."

"And vice versa . . . ?"

"Equally. Sexuality for human beings always requires 'humanization,' reflection, and work: how do I fulfill this dimension of myself in order to transform it into a real relationship of love and respect for the other person that gives the other person what I call 'life.' I either find a way of living my sexuality, or I am a prisoner of my own fantasies, my own desires, and I just look for someone who is going to respond, and use that person for myself. For me that is always the way of sin, for fundamentally it is already a negation of the person who is in front of you."

At last *sin*.

Sin is a notion I've always found troubling. As many of my Buddhistic friends are always eager to point out, sin *qua* sin does not exist in most Buddhist teaching. "Abuse of the senses" does occupy considerable place in some strains of Buddhism, as does correct and incorrect sexual conduct, but the Christian idea of sin is absent. The notion of "original sin" that formed the foundation of Augustine's condemnation of all desire as corrupt strikes most Buddhists as simply ludicrous. Or as the cartoonist Robert Crumb, who illustrated Genesis, put it, it's "primitive." For Brother Peter, it seemed to fall somewhere in the zone of "folkloric attachment," as does the offense of onanism, condemned across the Sumerian tribes who regarded it as a betrayal of the obligation to breed and populate.

But then, as with many of Brother Peter's dialogues, I found myself again returning to the medieval theologians to better understand how close or far he adhered to fundamental dogma. The thirteenth-century Italian Saint Bonaventure followed strictly Augustine's arguments—namely that the awareness of desire and consequent shame that came with the tasting of the forbidden fruit in Eden had corrupted all sexual acts. Clearly he departed from the arguments of Thomas Aquinas, but his reasoning yoked the corruption of sex to the more fundamental "sin" of covetousness and even acts of theft. When Eve plucked the forbidden fruit from the tree, she violated a divine order; worse she still held the key to divine knowledge. Before her teeth sank into the sacred fruit, the concept of "private property" was not existent, but by snatching the fruit she led our prelapsarian ancestors away from common universal sharing into a psychic and spiritual territory of individual ownership. To own property meant that by definition one was corrupted—was sinning—and that the more universal sin of covetousness would inevitably follow. To covet was to lust for that which was not one's own *property*. Lust, then, is a product of private ownership, which defines the corrupted state of man and therefore must be renounced.

Much of the basis of monastic communities lay in following the *Rule of Saint Benedict*, which aside from swearing a vow to chastity included the renunciation of private property. Few of the vows of poverty, however, have ever been about suffering or self-denial as such. Embracing poverty was rather about renouncing the sin of ownership. Of course, there have always been contradictions. The finest cognacs, we might recall, were created in the abbeys, as were the rich beers of northern Europe, and nearly all monasteries, male and female alike, maintained vineyards. (Only the dour Protestants—and not all of them—came to see the Last Supper as complemented by unfermented grape juice.) Some of the grandest tapestries covered the walls of monastic refectories, and in their cupboards could be found stunning gold and silver goblets. The ideal of renunciation was highly subjective.

The ideal and the actual were fully present in Brother Peter's deliberations, as present as the distinctions he made between the core of sacred practice and the affects of the church's folkloric tradition. Combing out these distinctions was not easy—for me or for him. Since he was obviously maintaining an active—if periodic—sex life, the most obvious question was whether he spoke of that in his confessions. Indeed, his second rendezvous after leaving my place was an uncertain assignation.

"So," I asked, "should it happen this evening that a physical encounter develops, won't you have to confess it?"

He grinned. "Certainly. I make ordinary confessions. In my vows I also say that, well, I've given my life to God—and in that gift I give all of my life, both sexual and emotional. I've had the genuine intention to keep [those vows]. I've not succeeded for the moment to realize them fully, but I never forget that [sexual celibacy] is a part of it."

"But you don't struggle to suppress your desires and your sexual activity?"

"I don't know if I can suppress them. One can transform them and move ahead little by little perhaps. I think more about an internal transformation than of suppression."

"That's a fine—not to say convenient—distinction," I said, adding, "You don't really want to quit having sex with other men at this point in your life?"

"Just now, at this time in my life? No."

"But," I answered, "if I understand the practice of confession at all, you say to your confessor that you've done something you shouldn't have, you make your apologies and ask for pardon, yet at the same time you're saying that you know you are not going to stop doing those same things. Isn't that a serious contradiction?"

"I would like to arrive some day at that level of perfection or to conform with what I've promised. When I'm going to get there, I don't know, OK?"

A long silent pause ensued, which seemed to leave me more uncomfortable than it did him. Perhaps as a professional confessor he was used to waiting. But his answers seemed unsatisfactory. To say that you have given your life with all its imperfections to an institution like the Catholic Church, while at the same time you more or less excuse your peccadilloes as a failure to arrive at the internal peace that would release you from them, struck me as somehow insufficient, too easy—both for him and for his confessors.

So, in a later conversation, we came back yet again to the matter of back rooms and what happens in them. I ought to confess this was a point of rupture I'd had years ago with a theologian from Catholic University on the NPR interview show *Talk of the Nation*. The theologian in question, eager to show the progressive face of his church, was ready to acknowledge physical relations between the same sex *in a committed relationship* as not necessarily "sinful," but when I proposed that so far as I was concerned sex bars and saunas were little different from sporting clubs where men—mostly—had a good time, he nearly hung up the phone. Brother Peter was less easily distressed, though aside from what he'd watch in his private DVD collection I was never sure that he had any real knowledge of back rooms or any overt sexual stews where the notion of attending patiently to your mate was as alien as asking your grandma to clean your dildo. The whole point of backroom group sex is the loss of structured social bonds in the pursuit of the abject.

Rituals of total abandon create zones in which we human animals dare to touch experience that transports us beyond ourselves and set aside Apollonian formality and restraint or Aristotelian reason, zones of behavior clearly outside the order of either Augustinian or Aquinian teaching, in which we dare to offer ourselves up in total physical sacrifice.

We moved on to an experience, one of my own, which also, subjectively, took on the character of a joint sacrifice and plainly touched some quality of being that was not simply physical.

"I'd like to speak of something that happened some years ago," I began, something that happened with an Irish guy. It was the beginning of an affair, which we both knew would not have an unlimited run but which all the same had grown alarmingly intense. The setting was one of the grand hotels of Budapest, the Gellert, which is attached to one of the grand baroque temples of eastern Europe, the Gellert Baths, which are even older and grander. No spa in prewar Europe could come close to competing with the Gellert for the elegance of its design, the nuanced control of its natural hot spring waters, or the refined quality of its services. (Remarkably, the spa survived Allied bombing during the war even while the adjacent hotel was severely battered.) Budapest, of course, is peppered with splendid spas, indoors and outdoors, some dating back a thousand years, even when it was ruled by the Romans, who called the settlement Aquincum after the name given it by the first recorded settlers, the Celts. My mission at the time was twofold: I was producing a long report for NPR on the history, culture, and health benefits of Europe's spas, and I was in hot pursuit of my recently found Irishman, and after all, who better than with a genuine Celt to explore this ancient Celtic curing ground?

I'd stumbled across this particular Celt some while earlier in the corridors of the same Dublin spa where a well-known Catholic priest had succumbed to a fatal heart attack *in flagrante delicto* as reported in *The Irish Times*. My Celt, though raised Catholic, was an explorer of several spiritual tendencies, and at the time he assured me, based on prior experience, that the same Dublin bathhouse we were enjoying was a regular destination for many holy fathers. When I mentioned my radio documentary project exploring several therapeutic spas, he was immediately interested, as he was also considering buying an investment property in Budapest. We arrived at the Gellert midmorning. Because I was visiting as a journalist, we were given a full and immediate tour by a comely guide who understood exactly what the two of us were about, offering us a warm wink as he left our room. Still a bit early for lunch or for a spa treatment, we decided to spend a while in the intimacy of our room. Rather quickly we found ourselves, to be indiscreet, "plugged into each other." Firmly. Intensely.

"Everything was advancing as imagined," I told Brother Peter. "Then, sharply, almost alarmingly, some still more intense sense passed between us. Like a bright, oval, spinning electrical charge. It wasn't about pleasure. It was absolutely something else. We had escaped our senses. Doubtless there are several neurological explanations. We looked at each other with fright but also with a mutual recognition that something had passed between us that neither of us understood, that seemed to be beyond our individual and separate selves. It was something I had never felt, and neither had he, but we understood that we had each experienced the same thing."

As I recounted my story, Brother Peter—he was clearly at that point *Brother* Peter—took on the manner of a confessor. "*Furcht*, the Germans call it. It's a kind of fright that Nietzsche wrote about. A terror of the sublime. Something that touches the sacred, something that sweeps over you, nearly like terror."

I'd hardly expected him to speak about Nietzsche. "But isn't that what we seek most profoundly in the idea of sacrifice, which to be genuine, must in some sense touch the sacred?"

Patiently, he shook his head. "I live as I believe, and that includes my sexuality when that happens. How I live my spiritual life is one thing. The other is there, I pay attention to it, the gift of the self, but not just to use it for pleasure. You pay attention to the sensation of the body's skin, of touch, not to make that the focus of relations, not simply for yourself. Sacrifice, to make it something sacred, is an offering. The Greek verb in the Gospels is *to employ* [or to put at the service of], meaning to present, to offer, to present at the altar the sacrifice you give to God so that it becomes pure or sacred, and in some cases what you have given could redound to others. There are different kinds of sacrifices."

"Rather different than offering yourself."

"You have the holocaust [in the generic sense of a burnt offering] in which what you offer is completely consumed in flame, that is, it's offered to God in its entirety with no expectation of return. It's only the smell of the smoke that rises up to God because odor or smell is the least material of the senses. For us Christians, it's the only thing that Satan cannot turn into a sin. All the other senses pass through the eyes, the ears, touch, taste, but odor is so immaterial that it cannot [be perverted], thus the contact with God passes through the sense of smell. In a holocaust offering, whatever the sacrifice is, you place it on the altar to be entirely consumed. You save nothing for yourself. There are other sacrifices to expiate sin, a small offering of blood on the altar. And then, of course, the famous Communion sacrifice, a part of which is given to God and a part of which is eaten by the human believer. All of that is in play in making sacrifices. You need to bear it all in mind or you risk not understanding (or being understood), but in every case [sacrifice] is a question of gifts, of offerings, and of Communion between man and God, or between men themselves, God remaining at that moment still at the center [of the offering]. That is what you search for and that is the function that sacrifice serves."

The pursuit of the ecstatic loss of self, the sacrifice of the self in the pursuit of the sublime, the sacrifice of the self in the cause of common commitment, the sacrifice of the self for a single other, none of these is particularly Christian and none need carry any particular charge to distinguish one sexual being from another. For Brother Peter and other believers, the act of ritual Communion is literally the sacrifice of one's own body and blood as it becomes divine and one with God/Christ on the altar, only to be reborn in the mystery of endless resurrection *within* the Christian Communion. Standard catechism.

But again what of the headlong pursuit of the abject, of the utter dissolution that comes with sexual rites of many cultures, be they the worshipers of Isis or the tribes of New Guinea or the genuinely heartfelt declarations of those who enter into a collective Dionysian sexual abandon, ecstatic beyond expression, walking at the rim of the abyss? Of Nietzschean "*furcht*"? Is that not also present in those who renounce the prudent and sane counsel of public health promoters who warn continuously always to make their sex "safe?" It is here that we enter the ultimate back room of self and selflessness, of the endless quest for the unity of the alienated one with the endless all, expressed as much by the longing pantheistic verses of masturbatory-soul in Walt Whitman's "Song of Myself" as in the more prosaic Freudian and neo-Freudian metaphors for phallic completion, flooded, as Whitman would have it, by the endless effulgence of transcendent longing and desire?

The bedrock of Brother Peter's practice rested solidly with Thomas Aquinas, who in the *Summa Theologica* explains the mystery of Christian sacrifice through the ritual of the Eucharist. Not merely a convenient memorial to Christ's crucifixion, as contemporary Christian *lite* would have it, the Eucharist for Aquinas—and for Brother Peter—goes much further than recollection. It is about entering what might as well be called a trance of ultimate pain and suffering in which we torture the victim only to become that victim. It is a theological terrain rife with fissures and volcanic eruptions that I am far from competent to explicate or enter. But for those who truly believe in the Catholic calvary, literal embodiment of the ultimate sacrifice is inescapable, an act in which we symbolically eat, are eaten, and are restored, or *transfigured and glorified* in order to enter into that spiraling circuit of total consciousness that knows neither beginning nor end nor material understanding. As the word suggests, it is the transmutation of the individual self that enters into total Communion.

Profane, blasphemous, as it would surely sound to most of the devout, that sense of total Communion is exactly what more than a few gay men say they seek—and a few claim to have found—when they give themselves over completely to the silent actions of sling rooms and bordello tables made famous and notorious in New York and Berlin, San Francisco and Paris. But it is an evanescent Communion, a Communion of the anonymous that finds in the instant of its ecstasy the evaporation of identity both personal and collective. Surely as profoundly as any time in my own life, those few seconds of *furcht* with my Irish mate back in Budapest took the two of us beyond any sense of separated self that either of us had ever experienced.

Perhaps the most profound, and provocative, deliberation on the collective search for the abject appeared at the very depths of the AIDS epidemic in an essay by Leo Bersani titled "Is the Rectum a Grave?" For many, maybe most, of my friends working in AIDS prevention, it was a scandalous document because it stepped aside from the safe-sex debate that they—and I as a journalist covering the epidemic—were so strongly propounding. Bersani's argument was complex and multilayered, but the title itself struck to the core of AIDS panic. Most gay men infected by HIV had taken in the virus through the walls of their rectums when other HIV-infected men had ejaculated inside them without having worn a condom. *On me—Not in me* was the slogan of the day. To be penetrated was to take the first step toward the construction of your own grave.

That was and remains inescapably true. But Bersani was interested in a larger death.

The first years of the epidemic brought to "the general public" the intimate, sticky details of just how gay men make sex. While all the school yard terms—*up yours, cocksucker, fudge packer, twinkle toes*—certainly alluded to one man penetrating another, the very fact that these were epithets to be tossed at your rivals also in some way drew a screen over the visual force of the act by which a wet glans pressed open the tight red ring of the anus. With AIDS that screen snapped open as the phrase *anal intercourse* spread through the airwaves and across the columns of the morning paper. Indeed, when my own use of the phrase *anal intercourse* became reasonably common on NPR, letters of complaint began to stream in from listeners, including one major Jesuit-owned member station in Cincinnati. Even some of the network's most famous political correspondents tried to kill my reports. One listener complained, "I don't need to hear about anal intercourse while I'm making blueberry pancakes for my son as he's preparing to go to school."

My reaction at the time was that if this Oregon mother's son was old enough to wonder what the words meant, then he especially needed to hear them so that he would understand very clearly how this disease was—and wasn't—spread. In another sense, of course, the child's mother was exactly right. The normalization of anal intercourse among men posed, and still poses, a profound challenge to the fundamental identity of the phallic Western male, a creature who, as the feminist writer Andrea Dworkin lamented, had established his commandeering power and authority directly and metaphorically through the weaponry of his phallus. *To be fucked* was, and is, to be abused and subordinated by the power and authority of another. It is such a common usage of daily language that we easily gloss over its roots when we say, "I really got fucked at the office today." We know well that the predicate does not refer to ecstatic *jouissance*.

To return to Brother Peter's formula for justifiable sex, we also know that neither does the phrase refer to the enrichment of human bonds within a loving pair. Leo Bersani's rectal grave addressed the representation of the shattering of phallic authority, the total relinquishing of the male self that all we males were raised to take as our privilege. It's a subtle argument that confronts both what we "safe-sexers" were saying and the liberal Thomistic argument made by Brother Peter. Jettison playful sex, anonymous sex, ecstatic communal sex, they both argue. Bring yourselves under the tent of normalized coupledom. Embrace monogamy. Even if marriage itself cannot be yours, behave as though you are married and subordinate your desires to the ancient models of husband and wife for whom the creation of a stable household formed the basis of civil community. Bersani calls it the "pastoralization" of sex that in effect reenacts the oppressive (and everywhere failing) model of the *Father Knows Best* nuclear family, a family model the hard right uses everywhere in the world to mutilate homosexual men and women. He argues that "implicit in the violence toward gay men (and toward women both gay and straight) *and* the rethinking among gays (and among women) of what being gay (and what being a woman) means is a certain agreement about what sex should be. The pastoralizing project could be thought of as informing even the most oppressive demonstrations of power." Most pathetic of all are the gay campaigners for normality who embrace a model that on the surface promises pastoral peace but beneath the picnic poster conceals the worst dimensions of dominion, oppression, and human subjugation.

For Brother Peter, who fiercely opposes extending the sacrament of marriage to same-sex lovers but endorses a sort of secular, laic equivalent (see chapter 5), Bersani's project rejects everything that liberal, humanist Catholicism requires. Bersani's sexuality is not a tool for the civilizing project, nor is his mission to redeem and rehabilitate the necessary act of penetration as gay activists would have it: "But what if we said, for example," Bersani writes, "not that it is wrong to think of so-called passive sex as 'demeaning,' but that *the value of sexuality itself is to demean the serious efforts to redeem it.*" Accept that being fucked is and must be demeaning, that it must constitute the degradation—the *inversion*, as the Victorians put it—of masculinity. In that act of self-abnegating submission, our male rectums become the locus in which the essential masculine subjectivity of pride dies—and "it should be celebrated for its very potential for death."

The death Bersani wants to celebrate is not biological death of the human organism, but the destruction of the "sacrosanct value of selfhood, a value that accounts for human beings' extraordinary willingness to kill in order to protect the seriousness of their statements. The self is a practical convenience; promoted to the status of an ethical ideal, it is a sanction for violence."

Bersani argues finally that while the sexual embrace may indeed reinforce, even concretize the humanizing solidarity of loving mates, to leave sex there and there alone is to misunderstand its other meaning for the human animal. That other meaning is not at all concerned with joint enrichment or community civility but with an equally powerful drive for the utter loss of the self—a destruction of the self that nearly all the great religions of the world present as an essential step on the ontological route to meaning and internal peacefulness. "Male homosexuality," he concludes, "advertises the risk of the sexual itself as the risk of self-dismissal, of *losing sight* of the self." The genuine and deeply dangerous *jouissance* of the ecstatic act is to take us to the very same destination Saint Augustine sought in the desert, as the Sufis seek in their whirling loss of conscious control, as the self-mortifying Hindu fakirs find on their bed of hot nails, as the Buddhist meditator finds in the chant of *no mind, no knowledge.*

CHAPTER FIVE

SACRED AND UNHOLY UNIONS

*In which Brother Peter and our
interrogator dissect the matrimonial cake.*

When at age forty-two my dear friend M. began buying copies of *Brides, Bridal Guide, World Bride,* even *Modern Wedding Cakes & Chocolates,* I began to worry. Militant antiwar protestor, civil rights activist, gay health counselor, and—briefly—flirtatious prospect, how was it possible that she had tripped into the trap of taffeta and lace? There were, of course, good legal reasons for her to take on a traditional matrimonial contract, not least securing vital rights for her soon to be foreign-national husband. Marriage throughout most of the world and most of recorded history has conferred both statutory and property privileges. But fine gowns and five-tier cakes?

The party was grand: outdoors in summertime on an antebellum estate surrounded by gargantuan oaks. A seven-piece—or was it nine?—band that kept everybody high-stepping until the stars captured the heavens and we had almost regained adequate sobriety to drive back to Washington. Hardly the only homo present, I remember nonetheless feeling the same gut-grinding outsiderness I'd felt at all the other weddings I'd been invited to, the worst having been the family affairs where presumably well-meaning but doubtful cousins and in-laws tilted their horsy heads, bunched their eyebrows, and probed. Surely my own glorious day would not be too far distant—*would it?*

"Heaven forefend!" I recalled saying once after gulping down every passing champagne flute I could reach. "*You might not find the bride to your taste.*" The tongue-blinded in-law was still struggling for an appropriate response as I excused myself, traded for a new flute on the passing tray, and made for one of the few kindred souls in attendance.

If funerals have always been at once bittersweet blends of loss and chattery picnicking, weddings have always given me effusions of controlled nausea. It's not that I bear ill will or bad tidings on those who've been swept up in the nuptial dance. The celebration of human bonding is surely one of the great triumphs of civilization, never mind the reality that marriage often proves to create more bondage than bonding, as exemplified by current divorce statistics or the record of wifely liquidations that were a hallmark of Henry VIII's reign no less than the punitive terms of Sharia. Joy is to be snatched wherever it can be found. And I would be the last to discount the value of community recognition of a genuinely joyous bond. My nausea arrives not even from the sense of being excluded, generally, as a same-sexer. My tendency to reflux arrives from the gas of anachronistic displacement; the ritual as commonly codified speaks to an era in which we, homo or hetero, do not live, and the manner by which we *do* live nowadays bears little if any relation to the terms of the legal contract.

Brother Peter, again, proved himself helpful in understanding my discomfiture. Hardly surprising, he is adamantly and unyieldingly opposed to granting the seal of *marriage* to same-sex couples. Equally, he is not especially happy extending the word *marriage* to what happens in a city hall office that registers conjugal relations between a man and woman. For his purposes the word entails not a fiscal relation, not a legal status, not the terms of property possession—all those fall under what he would regard as "folkloric" attachments to religious practice. *Marriage* for Brother Peter is and can only be a sacrament recognized and blessed through the divine mystery of the Mass.

Why? I asked.

"Because marriage is a commitment between a man and a woman whose purpose is the creation of a divine soul born in the image of God and created through a sacred physical union."

But what of those men and women who cannot "create a new soul in the image of the divine"? I asked.

He responded with a classical, priestly shrug, then added, "That the divine spirit is not realized biologically remains a mystery of God. But the objective of marriage in a Christian society must be to recognize a union which, in general, consecrates the continuation of humanity. That is not possible between two men or two women."

As was so often the case, I chose for the moment not to battle the logical lapses, the religious myopia, and the biological confusion in these assertions from a normally highly intelligent man. Who could possibly pass a high school biology exam and believe that the inability to conceive or bear children is a "mystery?" What possible sense of sociology or demography could assert that France, where fewer than 10 percent of the population are members of a Christian church, is today a "Christian" society? Even for those who cling to the notion that most French or Europeans are silent Christians, by what justification should a secular state be granted the right to apply the term *marriage* if that union rests within a sacred or divine ritual?

Without addressing these questions, Brother Peter turned his attention to the gay movement that wants to claim the term—and the right—for its own social and secular purposes: "What bothers me and has always bothered me in this debate is the sexual vindication that the gay groups always insist on."

"But wait," I said, "we weren't talking about sex. We were talking about the right to enjoy the status of married people. Even 'civil unions' or 'domestic partnerships,' as they're called in the U.S., are not restricted to sexual partners. They can be with a brother and a sister, an aunt and a niece or nephew, simply two friends."

"For me," he elaborated, "a civil union contract is not something based on sexuality. I think of those people, take for example two brothers and two sisters who remain celibate for whatever reason, who share their lives and maybe a house they've inherited from their parents, as I've seen in the countryside. I think we ought to envision a sort of civil contract that would not at all be a sort of carbon copy of marriage for the gays. It ought to be seen in much larger terms, in which if some people want to have a sexual relationship, well, that's up to them."

"But that already exists," I protested. "Even in America where there are domestic partnership laws, an aunt and a nephew can use [those laws], as can any other two people who want to commit to caring for each other."

But America was not on Brother Peter's mind.

"Do you know that in medieval society there existed contracts that permitted two men to become associated and treated by the law as if they were truly brothers, even including the option of passing inheritances to each other's descendants? That sort of contract absolutely does not bother me, but it's not written in the agreement that the two men must absolutely have a sexual relation."

"Yes, but that's simply one sort of contract within a specific theological tradition."

Aggravated, he went on.

"What I'm saying is, what business does the state, if it's a civilian, secular state, what business does it have in legitimating the sexual lives of adults?"

And there we came to the nub of the matter. Indeed what business is it of the state ever to confer favor or disfavor on our sexual acts so long as they are not abusive? For those who understand and believe that the union of bodies sexually is an act of divine engagement, let them so believe *among themselves* in whatever faith or personal code they have chosen to embrace. By what right should the state reject all the forms of polygamy and polyandry in the private sphere of the practitioners, whether it be in Edmund White's famous formula of the 1980s "banyan tree" model of a family of sexual brothers or the Mormon "family" model for populating the Utah desert, however loopy its underlying faith might seem to me? Further, by what foundation should *civil* contracts of aid, support, and inheritance be modeled on the current Anglo-European model of marriage that restricts the deal to only two persons, as nearly all civil union and domestic partnership contracts do?

Here is where I find Brother Peter's reference to the medieval model useful—even if it clearly undermines much

of the marriage campaign launched by the current gay movement, a campaign that has too often drawn on an unfortunate
and ill-constructed book written by one of the major medieval scholars of the last century, John Boswell. A gay practicing Catholic, Boswell chaired the medieval studies program
at Yale University. His book *Same-Sex Unions in Premodern
Europe* became, for a while, a virtual altar for the gay-mar-
riage crusade. In it Boswell drew on an array of documents
written largely in Latin and Slavonic (the language of the
Eastern Church) that were used in early ceremonies codifying
commitments between men and were conducted within the
church by priests and even bishops (though the term *bishop*
had a distinctly different meaning in the fifth and sixth centuries than it implies today). One ceremony he cites is especially suggestive of something that would seem to modern
eyes a sort of marriage:

i.

The priest shall place the holy Gospel on the
Gospel stand and they that are to be joined together
[hoi adelphoi] place their <right> hands on it,
holding lighted candles in their left hands. Then
shall the priest cense them and say the following:

ii.

In peace we beseech Thee, O Lord.

For heavenly peace, we beseech Thee, O Lord.

For the peace of the entire world, we beseech Thee, O Lord.

For this holy place, we beseech Thee, O Lord.

That these thy servants, N. and N., be sanctified with thy spiritual benediction, we beseech Thee, O Lord.

That their love [agape] abide without offense or scandal all the days of their lives, we beseech Thee, O Lord.

That they be granted all things needed for salvation and godly enjoyment of life everlasting, we beseech Thee, O Lord.

That the Lord God grant unto them unashamed faithfulness [pistin akataiskhynton] <and> sincere love [agapn anypokriton], we beseech Thee, O Lord.

That we be saved, we beseech Thee, O Lord.

Have mercy on us, O God.

"Lord, have mercy" shall be said three times.

After the ceremony, the two men each kiss the Gospel and each other, and the priest lifts the crowns, blesses them, and dismisses them.

What could be clearer, especially with the lifting of the crowns by the priest, a move also used in marriage ceremonies?

Boswell's book is packed with lengthy footnotes in Latin, Greek, Slavonic, and English, but he encourages the general reader, for whom he intended the work, to pass by all that as such details would only be of interest to "specialists." One of those specialists, another gay classicist, Daniel Mendelsohn, who writes regularly for *The New York Review of Books*, and has published three highly successful personal memoirs, did take a look at the notes and Boswell's translations. Mendelsohn's long critique of Boswell published in the journal *Arion* was devastating. Not only did Boswell draw selectively on his citations, but he also cooked his footnotes, mixing those in Greek with those in English, making it especially difficult to follow, and in Mendelsohn's reading Boswell obfuscated the real context of the ceremonial documents. Further, Boswell suggested that he had stumbled on these "secret" documents through the advice of a "correspondent who prefers not to be named," suggesting the risk of academic reprisal. Alas, as Mendelsohn points out, the documents were very well known to scholars, some of them as long as a century earlier. But worst, these same-sex union ceremonies had been overwhelmingly understood as *friendship* commitments that in no way suggested equivalence to the conjugal implications of marriage. Indeed, given both the Greek antecedents of such friendship rituals and the ascetic formulation of monastic and semimonastic friendship extant in the very secretive early church, and later following the doctrines laid out by Augustine, erotic union seems the least likely interpretation.

Mendelsohn, however, did not stop with Boswell's failures—and since Boswell was already dead from AIDS, no debate with the Yale professor was possible. Rather, and much more damningly, Mendelsohn took on the general gay professoriate, the by then and still now well-established and often celebrated gay men and lesbians who reign over many of the nation's gender studies departments:

> The failure thus far on the part of left and, espe-
> cially, gay intellectuals to respond with an appro-
> priately vigorous and public skepticism to Boswell's
> questionable methods and tendentious conclusions
> is, I think, particularly distressing—not least because
> it leaves the left embarrassingly vulnerable . . . The
> resistance to invoking rigorous standards of intel-
> lectual or aesthetic quality is the corrupt legacy of
> a high-minded commitment to eradicate oppressive
> hierarchies and to demystify claims to authority.
> It is one thing to acknowledge that we are all of
> us—scholars, critics, philosophers—implicated
> in the social, political, and historical contexts we
> inhabit . . . [but] it is entirely another matter to
> make this insight the basis for a wholesale aban-
> donment of what one historian called the "noble

dream": a common standard of methodological
and argumentative scrupulousness, if not actually
some elusive "objectivity," in historical, critical, and
philological inquiry.

Plainly put, the fierce struggle for acceptance of gays and
lesbians in the academy and for opening up scholarship
on homosexual themes had corrupted and degraded the
quality of their own intellectual mission. Faced with a gay
rights campaign dedicated to the cause of equal access to
marriage—and to military service—none dare question
the fraudulent scholarship by which one of their own had
sought to bolster the campaign. Mendelsohn's critique was
a damning attack on homo-scholarship, and yet it fell short
of what might have been a more profound critique on the
whole enterprise of the marriage debate. If Mendelsohn
clearly demolished the notion that these medieval ceremo-
nials were nothing at all like the marriages envisioned by
Adam and Steve, Beth and Betty, it still might have been a
propitious moment to ask what their function was. Clearly
one function appeared to be toward diffusing dangerous
conflicts between rich and important heads of households, a calming of clan conflict that could have quickly
turned bloody. Yet the ceremonies also, at least at times,
sought to recognize deep bonds of amity and solidarity
between individuals.

The key word in all the ceremonies is the Greek *agape*, used widely in ancient philosophy as well as by the church and defined usefully by theologian Thomas Oord as "an intentional response to promote well-being when responding to that which has generated ill-being," or more broadly, a love that goes beyond all explaining. Nothing in its usage presupposes sexual union—any more than it excludes sexual relations. Sexual union is simply another matter.

Which is where my conversation with Brother Peter began. Wholeheartedly he embraces the notion of civil commitment between human beings—possibly even more than two partners whose object is *agape*. It is a far larger notion than that subsumed under marriage, and at its best it proposes the bonds of solidarity that tied together the premodern family and served as a basis for civil society. While the personal care and nurture of one soul by another was a part of that pact, the communal pact itself reached far further than the limits of either the bedroom or even the modern sense of the nuclear household. Perhaps partly because I have a good deal of my own roots in the American South where the annual family reunion still persists in the countryside, and due to my civilly registered companionship now in France where my mate's extended family generally gather two or three times per year with no fewer than forty people at each sitting, it is increasingly clear to me how grave are the losses we have suffered at the hands of the modern, postindustrial nuclear family focused on the standard marriage contract. The simplest, most obvious measure is the Western divorce rate. Roughly half of American marriages end in divorce, while around 40 percent unravel in Europe. Indeed in France the distaste for marriage continues to rise as heterosexual couples increasingly opt for one of several civil arrangements that provide for tax relief and property protection.

(As I write these lines, the bishops and priests of France have taken to the streets in greater number than at any time in the last century. Why? The ruling Socialist Party, making good on a 2012 presidential campaign promise, has passed legislation that will extend all current marriage rights and privileges, including adoption, to same-sex couples. Yet no matter how many incense boats swing and twirl through the mostly abandoned churches of the nation, the population appears to care little who will slip between the reformed marriage sheets. Even arguments shared by some secularists against homo-adoption on the grounds that children need parents of each sex carry little resonance where more than a third of children grow up in single-parent households and some three hundred thousand are raised by same-sex parents.)

All sorts of arguments abound to explain the steady decline in traditional marriage, not least the necessity for each parent to work and the incumbent stress placed on the two working adults for child care, household maintenance, school support, and related "after-school" social events. As public investment in schools continues to decline both in Europe and the United States, those pressures grow only heavier. What then does all that have to do with homo-marriage and same-sex unions? For those who lack the human and financial resources to keep paid staff and home babysitters, the burden on the nuclear unit becomes, as countless marriage counselors have reported, unbearable. Ironically, it is largely among the poor and immigrant populations where extended families survive—largely composed of aunts, grandmothers, and single daughters but also including uncles and grandfathers. Those are also the populations who experience the most durable, if not always the most progressive, households. Surely then the challenge for all of us as human beings is to figure out how to recover the strength and psychological sustenance that the disappeared, archaic extended families provided to working couples, their children, and their aging members: how to restore that sense of *agape* that once formed the basis of our ancestors' commitments without the brutality and gender suppression that enabled male masters to treat their women and children as chattel?

The twentieth century's utopian experiments in resolving these ancient questions suggest, sadly, the dark consequences of planned solutions, be they the early Soviet efforts at redefining family and parenting roles or the communal models hatched in Northern California that all too often resulted in no parenting or in deadly messianic missions like Jim

Jones's Peoples Temple that terminated in the Kool-Aid cyanide deaths of nearly all its members. As the British political philosopher Isaiah Berlin famously argued, most enduring transformations in social behavior have emerged not from revolutionary theory and planning, but from incremental, pragmatic, daily self-reinvention by those people who have no choice but reinvention. For the homo-sector, Stonewall comes to mind: a rebellion whose time had come among a group of men who saw other rebellions against repression all around them and seized the moment. Less well appreciated are the families built of lovers and friends amid the falling cinders of the AIDS epidemic in the 1980s. These ersatz families, the ones Edmund White called banyan tree families, grew at once laterally and vertically from the lovers of former lovers, the friends and lovers of current lovers, into compacts of committed caregivers and bedmates whose motivating energy was personal and collective survival in the midst of plague.

As numerous writers have documented (most extensively by Jeffrey Weeks, Brian Heaphy, and Catherine Donovan in *Same Sex Intimacies*), it was a remarkable moment of pragmatic union that would have pleased the finest Feuerian utopians of the nineteenth century. From the death triangle at the heart of San Francisco's Castro District to the ordinary neighborhoods in Missoula or Lexington or Huntsville, new sorts of families beyond the limits of blood—though indeed virally linked by blood—arose. Those who survived the epidemic have in remarkable proportion survived the decades, the pall of death and the zest of sex having long disappeared. And often as not, it was the self-invented funereal ceremonies, many written in advance by the dying, much as Churchill designed and orchestrated his own funeral for the survivors of the Second World War, that became the consecrating events among them.

As that beleaguered generation has grayed and wrinkled, its dream has also faded. Everything from internet cruising to mastery of demographic niche marketing and indeed the global marketplace's thirsty appetite for homosales has undermined the sense of embattled outsiderness that gave birth to these newfound kinship networks. French Rail, IKEA, Macy's, Starbucks, American Airlines, Ford Motor Company, and scores of others have launched serious gay-directed ad campaigns. The effect, in many ways laudable, has normalized gay people while at the same time robo-mixing us all into the great consumer soup of individual wallets. The ability to pay, by cash or credit, has steadily replaced nearly all other measures of inclusion and exclusion in modern life. Disappeared in that glowing success story, celebrated by middle-class lobbying combines like the gay Human Rights Campaign, is the sort of creative bonding and kinship commitment that for a while promised to be the gay movement's single most creative contribution to the larger society of the West.

These "families of choice" celebrated with such romance and vigor in the 1980s and 1990s, complete with their own homespun commitment ceremonies, could hardly be understood as direct descendants of the "same-sex unions" that John Boswell tried to resurrect in his writings about the medieval church. They were, if anything, fuzzy reenactments of the nineteenth-century utopian communities that popped up all across New England and the Midwest; almost never did they carry any Christian perfume. Brother Peter's sharp distinction between the ancient monastic rites and declarations of amity and brotherhood and the intimate wedding cake rites so famously carried out in San Francisco's city hall was absolutely correct. Yet accurate as he was, there was something finally arid, too defensive, too internally divisive in his defense of official church doctrine. By reserving marriage as a sacrament that could be realized only within the context of the Mass, which in itself serves to consecrate, in his terms, the divine creation of new life, he also abandoned the mystery of Greek *agape* that transcends now and historically all these human unions. Neither were the parallels completely insignificant, and contrary to Boswell's strained effort to see the medieval unions as forbears of today's homosexual "marriage," the medieval friendship unions were nonetheless born of similar human impulses: Both sought social recognition for the spiritual necessity of personal solidarity within friendship; both sought to bind affection in the sense of *agape* with unqualified mutual care and responsibility; and both aimed to legitimate that solidarity to a larger and largely uncomprehending majority society. Conventional marriage in nearly all circumstances has staked out a far smaller secular mission, constrained and negotiated through a unitary power of church and state that ought to have died with the twin revolutions of 1776 and 1789. The market-thirsty individualism that has now become the bedrock of today's gay movement has, under the cover of sexual equality, perversely propelled us all backward into the brittle bridal cake of the premodern era.

CHAPTER SIX

A Band of Secular Brothers

*In which Brother Peter mounts the
motorcycle of Rainbow Camaraderie.*

When Brother Peter opened our first communication by asking if I always cruise priests, I might have answered, "Only when they look like they've just arrived on a Harley from the local leather bar." In his black leather jacket, boots, chain attached to Levis, he seemed to fit the profile.

To a large degree I wasn't wrong. While Brother Peter's primary family may be, as he told me, his monastic order, the broad network of gay motorcycle clubs has given him a parallel extended kinship network. Motorcycle clubs across northern Europe have become, at least in recent years, his gay contact grid. It was spring 2008 and he had taken the train back down to Paris to hang out with his moto-club buddies at Paris's annual Printemps des Associations, which you might think of as a country fair for all the LGBT clubs in and near Paris: the African Rainbow club, the homo swim team, the gay Rollerbladers, Rubber-Men, Melo-Men, Gay-Kitch-Camp, David & Jonathan (a Jewish gay group), and at least twenty-five more, not least of course the Gay Moto Club of Paris.

Confession: Until he told me about it, I'd never heard about the Spring Fair, though it is put on by the same city-wide organization that stages the annual Gay Pride march at the end of June.

"Well, you really missed something," he told me, his eyebrows arched as though in shock. "I went yesterday afternoon and everybody was there. Dozens of gays and lesbians for every taste, if you want to dance, make music, swim, do sports, hike, ride motorbikes, find sex. An incredible sense of conviviality. There's even a group dedicated to the memory of homosexuals deported [to the Nazi camps], AIDS prevention, the Sisters of Perpetual Indulgence, everything you could imagine. For me the thing I found the most interesting was that it wasn't all about the sex and porno world, back rooms and cruising bars or whatever, but this idea of . . . " He paused for a moment, lost for words. I began to wonder if tears might well up, but then he went on.

"I was talking with, um, I had a good conversation with the president of the Bikers' Club, which is something I truly like a lot. He's been with his boyfriend twenty, maybe thirty years. They're completely faithful. He sends out birthday greetings to all the members, organizes cocktail parties, dinners, outings . . . a real comradeship that's not based first and foremost on finding a sex-mate. That's what seems to me the most interesting part because it gives young guys the chance to hang out together in places where they can engage in ordinary activities, as everybody else in the world likes to do, without having to disguise or hide part of yourself."

It was one of the most touching moments I had with Brother Peter, for it was clear that, as complete as he found his monastic family, that family always required him to hide the critical piece of his identity that no one but his confessor knew about (or at least so he believed). A few weeks later he showed me photographs of one of those outings he had taken with the club to a park not far away where the monument was to a martyred saint. The men—the club is all male—stood before the monument in groups of three, four, five, their arms laced about each other's shoulders, fuzzy spring mist hanging like soft cotton swabs from the surrounding tree limbs.

The gay motorcycle clubs where Brother Peter finds succor and solidarity are not just party clubs. They are the sort of institutions that he would say help humanize the individual soul, not least because they speak to the particularity of being in a group of outsiders whose outsider status is never likely to disappear even in those lands where "gay marriage" becomes legal and homophobic attacks mostly disappear. Standing apart from the fundamental unit by which humans regenerate themselves *is to be outside*, no matter how many gay mommies and daddies show up on television sitcoms. How we address the state of outsiderness, both hormonally and socially, Brother Peter would argue, may offer us a fear measure of how deeply we are ready to engage in collective "self-humanization."

To illustrate what he meant, he told me about a rugby player in a town where he once lived.

"I was living then in, let's say a town in the East, well known for its obsession with rugby. Everybody, all the young men, played rugby. There was even a semiprofessional team. Well, several years ago one of the players decided to 'come out.'"

"To his family or to the team?"

"Everybody. It seemed OK at first. Nobody insulted him or attacked him, but immediately he could feel that his relations with the other guys on the team changed despite the fact that he had played with them for years."

"They wouldn't touch him during practice or what?"

"The other guys could no longer be natural with him because immediately there was a sense of uncertainty when he sought physical contact with them, when he touched them. Something had been broken in his relations with the rest of the team."

"How did *he* feel when he touched the other guys after he'd come out?"

"Ehh, I don't know. That's one of the problems, isn't it? Where is the ghetto? In our minds? In theirs? Both?"

I asked Brother Peter how he had counseled the young athlete whom he seemed to know.

"Actually, I never met him personally."

Too bad, I smiled with my eyebrows, but he didn't react.

"Later," Brother Peter continued, "the guy helped establish a gay rugby team that's done very well and still exists. I began to understand personally then that people have a need to discover a place for themselves where they can share things among themselves, even be a little bit cut off from everybody else. Still it also seems to me that while we can't mix everything that we are with others, why can't we be more open and accepting of different realities? Why do we have to live strictly . . . ?"

"Inside a group identity?"

"Exactly. These days when we have multiethnic teams with blacks, whites, Algerians, why do we have to have this sort of reverse discrimination? Nobody can be defined simply by the color of his skin or racial origins, so why should he be defined by his sexual orientation? That's something I have a hard time understanding."

The easy answer, of course, seemed rather simple: When any of us for whatever reason feels systematically excluded from the dominant culture, we tend to circle among ourselves for protection and self-understanding, for humor and for collective confidence. Ethnic minorities have always done so, from the Jews and Sumerians (or maybe even the Neanderthals at the hands of our ancestors) to the Slavs and the Croatians. Yet unlike all those linguistic and territorial human groupings, sexual dissidents have always cut across traditional boundaries, even discovering erotic attraction in the fact of their differences. Increasingly it is the same with monastic orders. Was it not a kind of search for identity that led Brother Peter himself into the monastery?

At first he thought it a ridiculous presumption. The Dominicans' founder, Saint Dominic, was moved to restore the faith of the Albigensian heretics to the official Church of Rome, and from there he and his followers continued as mendicant preachers across Europe, especially in the north. A band of preachers carrying the banner of the European world's most powerful institution, the Catholic Church, would seem to bear little resemblance to the scattered enclosures of sexual dissidents who came together to defend themselves against physical brutality and discrimination. But might we not remember that to proselytize has always demanded a structure of defense? Nearly all the monasteries through Europe's Dark and Middle Ages were protected by defensive walls *from which* they sent out their missionaries and *into which* they welcomed those in need of aid and care *so long* as the suppli-cants subscribed to the faith within the walls.

As the modern gay movement's most famous mission-ary, the martyred Harvey Milk, was fond of proclaiming, "We are out to convert your children." Milk's "conversion" was not to homosexuality but to a social—and some would say even a spiritual—recognition of homosexuality as a part of the human mosaic. Early on after his departure from New York to San Francisco, Milk understood that while he was at root a libertarian socialist with universalist ten-dencies, he also realized that he could succeed only if he stood within a community of his own kind, of gay men who were feverishly constructing their own permeable ghetto. Milk's dream, cut off by his assassination, was to realize a world in which those self-protective ghettos were no longer needed, would indeed wither away in the embrace of a com-mon humanity that was not, as Brother Peter says, "defined by sexuality."

The more I tried to understand what on the surface seemed like deep contradictions in his arguments, the more I realized I needed to understand the origins both of his sex-ual and his religious awakening. Not surprisingly, neither was without crisis and each was related to the other.

He began with the day of his ordination twenty-five years earlier. I wondered what he was wearing that day.

"I was dressed exactly as I am today—jacket and blue

jeans. The same as the day we met looking at the Pierre et Gilles paintings."

"You really remember that clearly?"

"Yes, because the celebration is very powerful. It marks your entry into the community. You arrive in street clothes. Your movements, your gestures, are very ritualized. You are prostrate, stretched out on the floor, arms forming a cross, in dialogue with the director of the community. You present yourself before him, and he is the one who gives you your religious habit. He places it on you. You don't touch it yourself, but he fits the great medieval tunic and belt over your pants and the shirt."

"Over your jeans?" I asked.

"Yes," he answered, understanding my not entirely proper curiosity about what lies beneath the holy robes. "You don't undress someone in the choir of the church. The celebration is for the public." Then he smiled—at last realizing the prurient double sense of my fairly clichéd question about what really is beneath those robes. "It's out of the question that you would appear naked in a religious rite . . . except for being baptized."

I explained that devout Mormons wear special undergarments that they are never permitted to fully remove, even when bathing. "A lot of people wonder if monks, like the Mormons, also wear special undergarments."

"After you've entered the religious life, you don't necessarily always wear pants under the habit. You can just put on briefs if you want. It's not important. There are many different outfits according to where and what country you're in, but you must understand that the taking on of the [religious] habit is a very ritualized act; it's very symbolic, very powerful, particularly for the people who are assisting, for the parents who have come to assist it as well, who are watching the total transformation of their son before their own eyes. It's a rite that often is accompanied by a change of name, and that genuinely presents his entry into a new identity."

Well, yes, that all seemed to make sense, especially for the parents who would be watching their son abandoning what it technically means to be male, not unlike a castration without the knife followed by a form of dress that to the ordinary eye seems to suppress any sense of gender or sexuality. How could it be less for the young man himself who is generally at the peak of his hormonal energy? And yet Brother Peter's description was flat. It—he—didn't seem to portray any deep personal transformation connected to the event, so I pressed further. I urged him to reenter each instant of the ritual. Little by little the timbre of his voice shifted, becoming softer and more remote.

"I often assist young brothers [in their ordination] and each time I relive my own [ordination] even if that sounds crazy to you: Each evening when you go to bed you take off the robe. You hang it on a hook on the bedroom wall. Then when you wake up the next morning what you see is this robe hanging on the hook." His speech now slowed and he permitted me, sitting there at my lunch table, to perceive the barest glimpse of the power of that matinal moment. He continued. "You slip it back on. You cover yourself in it. So each time you put the robe back on in the morning, you relive the first time you did it. You continue, you pursue what was begun the very first time."

The plain quiet of his voice was changing the man with whom I had played and whom I was struggling to know, as though he had entered a state of prayer reenacted within himself. It reminded me of a conversation I'd had with a neurologist who often works with dancers, who explained how the synaptic dance within our brains reenacts the memory of a dance that the body had performed or even witnessed. Memory, especially memory of powerful events, is never static or passive within ourselves. Deep recollection demands that our brains re-create the electrical chemistry of what we have done even though in each "repetition" there is always a slight alteration. How could prayer, any less than the performance of music or dance, be otherwise? That surely seemed to be what Brother Peter was undergoing as I sat a finger's touch away from him. The words spilled out of him, and he seemed to be taken back literally to the first time the medieval robe had slipped down over his shoulders, and he was, if not "reborn," irretrievably altered and sent forth on a new track. The coarse white cloth draped over the shoulders, the sacred scapular, the white belt tied around the waist: all these denoted the purity of life, and they were matched by the black hood worn outside, symbolizing the death and mortification of the sacred body, that demands penance.

The black leather he wears with the gay motorcycle club is as starkly apart from his monastic habit as is the decorated robe worn by the Sister of Perpetual Indulgence who plays hedge fund trades on her day job. And to the outsider, his life within the monastery is as different from his "street life" as a medieval peasant's is from a San Francisco opera diva's.

He went on with his daily ritual in the monastery as my mind kept floating from neurology to motorcycles to drag queens to hedge funds.

"I have my own room in the monastery's living quarters. The alarm goes off. I lie in bed listening to the news to know what's going on in the world. I take my shower and a coffee. Then, the moment when I put on my robes and attach each element of the habit, I've entered into my monastic brotherhood."

"And at that instant you are back, prostrate on the stones before the prior on your day of ordination? And back at that first time, you had no trepidation, no doubt about what was happening to your life, your future?"

"No, just the contrary. [I had] the sense of being sent into the void, the unknown, to find life. I had no idea where I was going but I knew I had to go there, that someone had called me to that life, without at all knowing what it was. It's something you cannot imagine in advance. Sure, I'd met the brothers, I'd visited several communities during my study. I had eaten together with them, but . . . " He shrugged.

Brother Peter was twenty-five years old at the time of his ordination—as he said, far from a boy but neither a fully developed man. He had begun his preparation for the monastery four years earlier, but then midway through he took a break and left for three years to teach, first in Brazil and then in Senegal. He told me his departure had not come from doubt but to test himself against the certainty of his initial decision to join the order. The brothers with whom he had undertaken his religious studies encouraged him to go away and reflect.

"They wanted me to be certain that I understood what my decision meant: that I would no longer control the decisions of my life, that the community would tell me what sort of work I would do, that it would not necessarily be what I had studied for, that when you take on a religious life, you can make no commitments, no promises. You have to understand how completely you are going to break with your old life, your old professional training, with family, love, children."

In fact, at the time he took his vows he was deeply in love. It was a love that at the time provoked no internal crisis, but later it plunged him into years of psychiatric counseling. It was his first attraction to another man and he was only eighteen when it began. Stranger yet, it was a chaste love—at least at the beginning.

"He was a priest," Peter began. "Twenty years older than me."

"But you said it was chaste? There was no physical contact?"

"Yes . . . but very little."

"Falling in love with another man at that age didn't provoke a crisis in your own sense of yourself as a man?"

"Curiously, no. Not then, at the beginning. The crises came much later. I was in love. I was in love with him. It was tender, loving. The affection I felt for this man came almost naturally—no, it didn't pose any real problems for me at that time."

"No sense of guilt over 'unnatural acts?'"

"No, but maybe that's because I come from a nonreligious family where there were no regular references to the church or its moral instruction. I never heard anything positive or negative about homosexuality, which really didn't exist in the countryside or in my parents' experience. So, it didn't seem like a problem because it didn't exist."

"It wasn't something people imagined?"

"No, you just didn't know."

"Not even schoolyard catcalls like 'dirty queer' between different kids?"

"Sure, but in those days I had the same attractions as all the boys and girls in class. Until I was seventeen I looked at girls, and it was girls I was interested in. The day I suddenly came across this man I was literally bowled over in place."

"You'd never even thought of caressing or kissing a guy before, even subconsciously?"

"No."

"So it was another radical, instant transforming moment, like the moment you felt what you said was a call to religious service?"

"Exactly."

Brother Peter stopped talking, and I wondered if he wanted me to turn off the recorder because these details, these memories, were too personal, too intent. I reached to the recorder. He took my hand and stopped me. It was not only OK to continue, but also he seemed to need to enter this deeply personal territory that either he had never spoken about before or that he wanted to be sure I would write about.

"I've had many transformations in my life. Each time I've moved, I've been uprooted. There was the total shock of my religious conversion when from one day to the next I passed from no faith to the fact of having God a living presence in my life. So, you see, these were more than 'transformations;' they were profound ruptures in the life I'd had before that forced me to pass utterly and nearly without any transition from one state to another, from one way of living to another. My religious transformation was really a consequence that came as a result of this love.

"Later, when I went abroad, that was another rupture in my life, as was my return, because I'd become deeply attached to the schools and the people where I was teaching. Returning to the religious life in Europe that I knew I had to follow was a heart-wrenching experience."

Brother Peter took up his religious studies four years after the affair began with the older priest. Their physical relations started slowly, long after the instant emotional attraction. It was, he insisted, his first genuine attachment, and while the older priest returned his affections, mostly as caresses and embraces, there were occasional sexual experiences when they lay together. But if it felt "natural" and "normal" to the younger man who would later become Brother Peter, it came to feel more and more unnatural to the older priest.

After Peter returned from his foreign sojourn and took his vows, he at first believed that he and the older man had reached a sort of accommodation.

"Because I was really in love and it was my first love, that love gave me a sort of peace with myself. I didn't feel any particular sexual need at that time. I was in love with a man. My heart was quiet. Everything was good. I took my first vows. Then the following year the man I was in love with fell into a nervous depression so profound that he broke off all relations between us. It was for me a terribly violent break.

"During vacation that summer I went to stay with close

friends of my family. This man [the priest] lived in his parish not far away, and I went there to see him, as I had left some of my things at his place. I'd told him when I entered the Dominican community that I would return to get my things. When I arrived at his house, everything was locked up.

"He'd left a note on the door that read, 'Go home.' Just that. Nothing else."

It was then that the worst crisis of Peter's life began.

"That night I drove home. The rain was pouring down. I was driving a small truck. And I was looking at . . . nothing. Nothing, nothing, nothing. I cannot understand why I did not have an accident. I was really completely destroyed. Lost. I felt empty.

"Then, a few months later, for the first time of my life, one night, coming back from a friend's house, I made a detour to a roadside where men were cruising. For the first time in my life I picked up a guy. A stranger."

As Peter recounted the whole experience, events that had taken place more than two decades earlier, his voice took on the same timbre he used when he recalled the day of his ordination and the taking on of the robe. There was a flatness to his speech, no particular drama, no sense of imminent tears. Rather it was as though he was a player in a Fellini film watching the rushes while they were happening.

A few weeks after he returned in the rain to the monastery, his personal belongings arrived in a plain package. No note. No return address. He never again spoke to the man who was, as he tells it, the only great love in his life.

"After that, sex came back very strongly in my life. My desires. My need. It was really terrible."

"You had already taken your vows?" I asked.

"The first vows, yes, but not the solemn vows. And the problem goes with the solemn vows, because really I am sure in myself that God . . . Well, I am a priest and a monk in a congregation. I discovered this problem of my sexuality, but, I had made the solemn vows. I think it was six months later I had a nervous collapse. I could no longer accept myself, who I was. I began finding ways to have sex from time to time whenever I had an hour away from my work. The easiest way, the most practical was to go to saunas. It was the worst time of my life and also the beginning of the AIDS epidemic here. I was convinced that I had to have been infected, which was going to be a terrible scandal. It was horrible. I wasn't sleeping. I wasn't eating. One night I seriously thought of throwing myself off the roof of the church. I didn't know how to go on."

For any priest to commit suicide is a far more grievous sin—and thereby would have provoked a far worse scandal—than being revealed as gay or having violated the vows of chastity. But for a monk, and particularly a young Dominican monk, to contemplate killing himself touches a profound betrayal of the order. Aquinas, still the greatest of Dominican theologians, wrote directly on suicide in the

Summa Theologica: "Every man is part of the community, and so, as such, he belongs to the community. Hence by killing himself he injures the community." How Brother Peter managed to mount the church roof, how he climbed down, how he managed to calm himself in the hours afterward, are memories that have disappeared but for a few broken fragments of recollection. None of his fellow monks except one who was a nurse knew what had happened. A doctor who was outside the monastery but cared for the brothers administered sedatives and other drugs. In time Brother Peter spoke to his confessor of what had happened, including the broken relationship with the older priest.

"I undertook psychological work trying to understand it all," he said. "It took a very, very, very long time. Years passed that were truly hard. It's not one of the things you can talk about to the rest of the community of brothers. It's not possible. It's a terrible burden to go alone and to try to find a personal path and then to finish by accepting who you are. That God exists is not the real problem. I have a spiritual relation that is my own, fundamental and exclusively my own, by which I want truly to serve the Catholic Church as a priest. I believe deeply in what I do as a priest. I believe in the grace of sacraments, in their spiritual power. I believe absolutely in all that. At the same time I know that there is a part of me that is human, which needs friendship and tenderness."

"And physical tenderness?" I said.

"Physical. Yes, it can be sexual or not, that doesn't matter."

"To be touched?"

"Exactly. The problem is to find those people who can understand this division, this doubleness. The others in my congregation do not understand my need of physical tenderness and friendship because it doesn't enter into the system [of their belief and practice]."

"You're sure of that? Sure that there are not others, straight or gay, among the religious congregation?"

"I don't want to know if there are," he said. "It doesn't interest me."

"Even to enrich their own psychological understanding as preachers?"

He began to grow impatient with my questions. "It's not my business. People I come across in the gay milieu do not genuinely understand what the spiritual life is about, this faith, or why I belong to this church that is reputed to be completely gay. Sometimes that can be very destructive. It's not simple. The danger for me—and it is a real danger—would be to have sex just for sex, going to those places that are only for sex. It's a danger because finally you risk becoming completely addicted to it, like a drug."

He shook his head at me. He wanted to be sure that I genuinely understood what he was trying to say.

"Then to find a friendship with someone who can understand that I can never live with him as a couple, that my religious life, the celebration of Mass, my community, will remain my priority. Some fellows have tried, but it makes things very, very difficult. So now I am, maybe, a little more distant regarding all that, much less interested in that quest than when I was truly looking for someone. Today I'm no longer there. If I meet someone and that person proposes friendship, I accept. But I explain from the beginning who I am and that that will not change. If they can accept that, OK. If they cannot . . . well. But that cannot change. If I broke my vows I know that it would destroy me. Completely."

Not until several weeks later when I relistened to our conversation did I understand the full measure of what Brother Peter had confided. Much of it he had already said, little by little, to his confessor and perhaps as well to the psychologist. But I realized as I listened to the silences, to the pauses, to his controlled inflections, that there was much that he had not said before and certainly not to a gay man. A part of his intention was surely to repeat the warning he'd made to me on our first encounter, that he was *not available* for a relationship, which because of my own existing relationship I had easily brushed aside. But in this fuller recounting of his life, he clearly needed to speak of his own duality, his absolute need of physical tenderness and spiritual mission, to someone who was specifically not of his spiritual community. Perhaps, too, this lay confession came of another sort of spiritual need, something that he had to hear himself saying free of the robe and far from the structured confessional of his order. That it was to me was of no particular moment or meaning beyond his judgment that I could be trusted not to violate his privacy, not to put him again at risk of losing the rock of his spiritual existence without which, as he said, he would be destroyed.

In a subsequent conversation several months later I asked him how his own journey had affected his role as a priest when he encountered other troubled gay men.

"It happens every now and then, but not often," he said.

"But when it does, do you feel then that you have in some way to distance yourself from your normal role as a priest and counselor?"

"No. When you take on the role of being a religious advisor, you have to pull back, keep yourself very much in the background. What's important is the person before you, how that person reacts. You must listen to his, or her, own life path, his psychological state, what he's able to accept internally. Sometimes it's happened that I felt they did not accept who they were, that they were making terrible self-judgments, and that what they were looking for was a priest who would condemn them for who they were."

"And how did you respond?"

"I try always to calm them down, because you must never judge, you must never condemn yourself."

CHAPTER SEVEN

THE BURNING FLESH
OF THE IMPURE SOUL

*In which our inquisitor descends toward
the flames of heresy.*

Following the counsel of a long-time gay friend and former colleague who nearly entered an American Dominican community, I brought up one day the untidy matter of
the Dominican role in the Catholic Inquisition. I'd assumed
Brother Peter would acknowledge that like all faiths and ide-
ologies Dominican Catholicism harbored its own faults and
frailties—not to say bloody crimes.

I was wrong.

We were again seated across from one another, but I hadn't
yet turned on the recorder. His reaction was visceral.

"Most of what has been written about the Inquisition is not true," he said, as though to close the subject.

Startled, even shocked, I gave him a perplexed stare.

Thousands of Spanish Jews and Muslims were obviously slaughtered in Spain and later in Portugal. Many whose names were well known were burned alive at the stake. Nearly the entirety of the Cathars, who'd were condemned by Rome during the Albigensian heresy, were liquidated in what was then Occitan and is now the Languedoc region of France. The church's complicity—and particularly the Dominicans' direct role—is hardly at question. The Knights Templar, once the bankrollers of Philip the Fair, were wiped out in a matter of months starting at dawn on October 13, 1307.

"Very little took place in France," Brother Peter insisted and added, as though to drive a spike through the myth. "All these histories of the Inquisition were anyway written by Anglo-Saxons."

We were on this occasion in France where categorical broadsides against "the Anglo-Saxon tradition" and "the Protestant mind" are as common as buttered snails. It is routine in the elite newspaper *Le Monde* or on the high-tone public radio channel France Culture to find putatively intelligent "philosophes" lumping together all Protestants—from fundamentalist evangelicals working in Africa to high Lutheran liberals in Minneapolis to strict Calvinists in Scotland to Gospel preachers of the Mississippi delta. Similarly so with "Anglo-Saxon economics." During one dinner party in 2009 a Parisian friend of forty years declared that only in the Catholic-heritage nations could one find such universalist social protections as unemployment insurance and national health care, programs that in fact began in nineteenth-century Lutheran Germany, postwar Scandinavia, and Anglo-Saxon Britain. But to hear an intellectual monk embrace the same appalling ignorance left me a little stunned.

Brother Peter reserved his worst venom for the Cathars. "Do you know how brutal and vicious the Cathars were?" he asked me before launching into a diatribe about the savagery and degradation they had, in his view, imposed on the poor peasants of Occitan. I did not; indeed few nonspecialists today have but the slightest notion of who these deep dissenters to Vatican authority were, though occasionally the rebel guerilla vintners of Languedoc cite their Cathar ancestors when they periodically blow up EU tankers bringing in cheap, imported wine. Indeed it was imputation of the Cathars' allegedly wanton homosexuality that the church used to destroy the movement from the first bloody attacks in 1208 and lasting for two more decades until the Treaty of Paris in 1229 dispossessed most of France's southern dukes, counts, and viscounts.

Certainly to a modern rationalist the Cathars were on the outer fringes of spiritual millennialism. Like most Manicheans they believed the universe was ruled by competing deities: the God of whom Christ was born, and the devil, who made and governed the physical earth including the flesh. The sacred, pure soul was therefore trapped within an essentially corrupt body, and that body was not corrupt simply because of the fall from grace in Eden, but because the flesh was itself made of evil. By comparison, Saint Augustine was a soft liberal. Like the Shakers who would emerge in America six centuries later, the Cathars declined to procreate. Females lived and worked in this sinful world with females. Males, mostly proselytizing, traveled the sun-dappled South only with males, usually two at a time—and hence the subtext arose for their eventual denunciation as depraved homosexuals and their destruction by an alliance between the church and the kings of France.

Unlike American Shakers, however, Cathars were more than a bizarre sect decorating the fringe of Christendom. Their sponsors and defenders included many of the most powerful lords and merchants from Toulouse to Albi to Carcassonne and back along the Mediterranean coast to Béziers on down into the hill towns of Tuscany. Their lands were rich and productive and their growing allegiance with lace and grain merchants gave them a weight that many other spiritualists lacked. Their ideas about property were as counter to convention as their theology. They declined to pass their lands from one generation to the next since property, like all physical matter, was of necessity evil.

The hierarchical Church of Rome, whose cathedrals were increasingly bedecked with gold and jewels and whose real estate holdings were the most extensive in Europe, they held equally suspect. And worst of all to the Catholic hierarchy, they forthrightly denied the sacraments of the Pauline Church, including of course the office of the Mass and the taking of Communion.

The Cathars were far from alone in their rejection of the material church. There were dozens if not hundreds of isolated dissenter communities—Bogomils, Paulicians, Arnoldians, Waldensians, Fraticelli, Spiritualists to name a few—that sought to return Christianity to the humble, mystical origins of its earliest years when believers sought salvation by rejecting worldliness. Many of the Cathars came from the East, particularly the Byzantine lands of modern Bulgaria (from which also came, according to certain etymologies, the verb *bugger*). Even within the sacred orders, including some within the Benedictine and Franciscan fraternities, there were strong movements for a return to purity in faith and practice. But none had gone so far as the Cathars, whose name in the Occitan language translated as *purity*, nor had any others so directly challenged both the sacramental and politico-economic order.

For the pope, the bishops and the royal authority of France itself, this double threat was something that could not be tolerated. It also touched the limit, I quickly discovered, of how far a man like Brother Peter nearly a thousand years later was willing to depart from tradition. Those who led the extermination of the Cathars were his direct spiritual forbears, most importantly Saint Dominic—a detail of monastic history I'd frankly forgotten on the day I broached the topic of Inquisition. Still, to understand the ruthlessness the Dominicans employed in suppressing these diverse "heretics," we have to recall the context without forgiving it. No one has captured the dark chaos of that medieval world more vividly than Umberto Eco in *The Name of the Rose*, where a bizarre mendicant called Salvatore describes swarms of dispossessed peasants who swept across north Italy and southern France at the beginning of the thirteenth century, drawing together an anarchic army of thousands who murdered, looted, and sometimes cannibalized all those in their way, from priests to merchants and all too often entire communities of Jews:

> We burned and looted because we had proclaimed poverty the universal law, and we had the right to appropriate the illegitimate riches of others, and we wanted to strike at the heart of the network of greed that extended from parish to parish, but we never looted in order to possess, or killed in order to loot; we killed to punish, to purify the impure through blood. Perhaps we were driven by

an overweening desire for justice: a man can sin
also through overweening love of God, through
superabundance of perfection. [p. 384, Vintage
edition 1998]

The inquisitors, *Domini canes*, or dogs of the Lord, as the
Dominicans became known, went far beyond the order's
original and current call as preachers who would travel widely
spreading the Gospel of the New Testament. Their initial mission was to spread the philosophical and theological teaching
of their greatest intellectual, Thomas Aquinas. They were formally established as the O.P. (Order of Preachers) in 1216,
the final year of Pope Innocent III's reign. For a Europe that
was largely populated by illiterate peasants living in caves or
forests and only at times elevated to the status of peasants toil-
ing in the seigniorial system of lords and dukes, the preachers
spread both the fear of eternal damnation for the nonbeliever
and the dream of salvation for those who accepted Christianity. Most of the faithful in any case were old and worn out
by age twenty-five and dead before thirty-five. As the British historian and geographer Graham Robb has exquisitely
shown, ordinary life was so mean and brutal that men regularly prayed to be stricken by a deadly disease that would
relieve them from their daily suffering. Women, who then as
now lived longer, were left to care for the children and grand-
children and tend scant gardens of rutabagas and other roots.

Trouble arose from the stark and plainly visible disparity between the bitter lives of the masses who were told to follow the path of the Christ and the ever-more glittering richness of the churches, abbeys, and cathedrals that were literally clothed in gold leaf. From within that vortex came the Franciscans, who followed the work of the Italian Saint Francis of Assisi. The Franciscans embraced the ideal of poverty as the root of Christian truth and maintained that Jesus and his apostles were history's finest exemplars of an idealized precommunist practice of penitence and humility. While the Franciscans skillfully avoided open challenges to the church hierarchy, its plump abbots and its bejeweled bishops, they regularly spun off legions of more radical spiritualists of whom the Cathars were the most hated. The ensuing power struggle turned as vicious and bloody as any in religious history. The Dominican preachers quickly emerged as the Grand Inquisitors who sentenced all those whom they deemed heretics to the *auto-da-fé*, or death by being burned alive. The mere fact that the accused did not survive the flames was plain indication of their impurity and their early admission into the mouth of hell.

Heresy was defined as a matter of false faith, which implied that they were also followers of satanic beliefs. But practice was equally important—and aside from failure to perform the sacraments in the manner prescribed by Rome, the most common evidence of evil frequently centered on sex. It mattered little that popes and numerous cardinals more or less openly maintained their own courtesans: for the Dominicans, women were defined as abject "vessels of evil," contact with whom not only soiled the monks and the clerics, but also, even worse, subjected them to damnation. However, with proper confession the preacher could win forgiveness, though the indiscreet "sorceress" who was supposed to have ruined him often found herself at the stake.

So it went for the individual sinner who had besmirched his robes. But for those who were damned as collective heretics, the broader accusation of committing "crimes against nature" was proclaimed. The Albigensians, the Paulicians, the so-called Bulgarian Bogomils, the Cathars, and perhaps most notoriously the Knights Templar (who some insist continue to survive disguised as the banking gnomes of Zurich) were all at one point or another denounced and/or damned by the Dominican inquisitors for acts of sodomy. There were hardly ever any witnesses, and nearly all the "confessions" came from the allegedly impure who were threatened with having their testicles ripped off by red-hot tongs, their nipples seared, their noses cut away, all in the name of establishing sacred truth; often the torture was performed even after confessing to collective heresy.

The Templars, who were founded by a handful of French knights in 1118 and won glory for their defense of the first and second Crusades of 1147 and 1190, finally fell from grace under Philip the Fair (whose own dalliances with fair young soldiers were also widely alleged) when they were judged to be a dangerous army of more than fifteen thousand with no external enemy to fight. Their fortunes waxed and waned for two years until Pope Clement V formed an alliance with the French king in 1307 and ordered them all arrested. Within the charge of heresy came the precise accusation that Templar initiation demanded of each young knight that he kiss the order's leader first on the mouth, than on the head of the leader's penis, and finally on his anus—clear and incontrovertible evidence for the Dominican inquisitors of the Templars' devotion to sodomy—evidence obtained, as with most Inquisition confessions, by torture. The definitive end of the Templars came when Jacques de Molay, the order's grand master and a former dining mate of Philip the Fair, was burned alive on March 18, 1314.

The Dominican inquisitors were no less harsh on their own when allegations of sodomy arose. One of the most famous cases concerned Antoine Richardi, a lieutenant inquisitor in southwestern France who was then himself charged with sexual offenses and roasted at the stake—in the mid-sixteenth century. The Dominicans' attachment to the *auto-da-fé* for sexual and theological heresy continued well into the seventeenth century as the European church faced ever-growing challenges from internal divisions and the Protestant reformation. French and Nordic Dominicans were far less aggressive in damning and slaughtering their enemies than were their Spanish counterparts, who had won encouragement from Columbus's sponsors, the royal couple Ferdinand and Isabella. Still, Toulouse, the primary seat of Dominican power, remained the most important launch site of the French Inquisition.

Seen from the twenty-first century, slaughter in the name of faith ranks as the most damnable charge against organized Catholicism. For many of the fallen-away Catholics I've known, the church's well-documented if sometimes exaggerated history was more than sufficient cause to reject it outright. The mere fact, some have told me, that a man like Brother Peter would have been summarily roasted if not first ripped apart by red-hot pincers ought to have driven him away from any attachment to Catholicism and even more so from the Dominicans. Yet it did not. It would be easy to dismiss his minimization of Dominican culpability as a manifest act of bad faith since he is a scholar and preacher versed in several modern and classical languages. The easy explanation, however, is usually simpleminded, as any reader of Umberto Eco's writings on the same era is forced to acknowledge.

One day as we were walking along a canal in the north, I asked Brother Peter about a friend he had often mentioned to me, a man from the Middle East who had given up Islam to embrace Buddhist practice—a double *infidel* in the language of the Dominican inquisitors.

"Do you believe your friend will face eternal damnation in the fires of hell?" I asked.

"Of course not," he said, as though I'd asked if his friend were a horned beast.

"But isn't that the message of John 3:16?" I said, paraphrasing the famous verse promising that whoever should believe in Christ would not perish but have everlasting life.

"Jesus never said that those who did not believe in him would perish. He only said that those who did believe would *not* perish. It's not the same thing."

"But for centuries preachers have said exactly that from their pulpits."

"Preachers in your country have also said that blacks and Indians are animals. Even your Constitution did not treat them as humans. Does that mean that's what you believe as an American?"

It was clear where the logic of the conversation might go, so I confessed straight out.

"Yes, of course, my ancestors—even my great-grandparents who were slaveholders—contributed to a crime against the humanity of Africans. And I would also agree that the European and American slaughter of North American Indians was very possibly the greatest genocide of human history. But while I find much that is good about the American idea, I don't preach the American cause."

I feared I was entering unstable ground, but Brother Peter's answer was mild.

"I don't preach what other interpreters of the Bible may have said or done. I preach the message of Jesus as we know it from the scripture."

"And so your Buddhist friend?"

"Like all kinds of people all over the world, if he is a good man—and I think he is—and if he is pure in heart—as I believe he is because I know him well—his eternal salvation should be no different than mine." He paused and looked at me kindly, but intensely. "Or yours . . . if you are pure of heart."

CHAPTER EIGHT

THE ETERNAL FLESH
OF THE PURE SPIRIT

*In which Brother Peter and our inquisitor
enter the canals of the mysterious spirit.*

By late spring it was clear that our dialogues, and very
likely our encounters, were drawing toward completion.
It wasn't because we had exhausted all that there is to say about
all that links the physical to the metaphysical, and we had not
exhausted the attractions both physical and metaphysical that
had drawn us to pass time together. Rather it was that these
increasingly formalized conversations had taken on a form of
their own. They had become in some sense a rite of passage, and
all rites of passage have beginnings and endings.

The natural conclusion to these dialogues was clearly the matter we had touched on only lightly in our penultimate encounter—the passage of our bodies through the terrestrial sphere. What had begun with crucifixion—the nailing of Saint Peter upside down onto his cross—should surely conclude with how a modern mortal understands his own ultimate passage.

"What do you really mean," I asked, "when you speak of life without end?"

"That as Jesus told the apostles they would be reborn at the time of judgment into eternal life."

"And you believe that? Literally? Like the story of Jonah in the belly of the whale?"

"I live in the faith of God as Jesus told us in the Bible."

"But you don't take that promise as metaphor, as a promise of emergence into something like the endless light of the eternal universe?"

He gave me that old smile of incomprehension, but I persisted.

"You believe that you will have this body that I see and that now I'm touching and that I penetrated and that penetrated me. You believe you will live in this body for timeless eternity."

"Certainly, yes."

"But which body? The one I see and feel today with its scars? The skin—sorry to say it—that's a little less tight beneath your chin and certain other zones? Or the muscle-toned body you had as a young soldier?

He sighed with a pluff. "These are not serious questions. They are the concerns of humans on earth, not of God."

We continued on in several minutes more of silence.

"I have to be going now," he said in the more formal voice of Father Peter, displacing both the intimate timbre of Brother Peter and the mildly salacious tone of just plain Peter.

As we parted I said, "Till the next time, then," and gave him a light kiss.

"Perhaps," he answered, his hands gripping my shoulders. And then he left.

Later that evening I recounted the exchange to Christophe, who had spent more than a decade of his youth in catechism classes. He was not impressed. "It sounds like a priest's remark," he said. "You didn't push him any further?"

"No, not yet."

Christophe scrunched his eyebrows, a gesture meant to close the topic.

The physicality of salvation is neither new nor incidental to Christian believers. Anyone who has passed beneath the Sistine Chapel and glanced upward toward Michelangelo's *Last Judgment* where the saved rise into the light and the damned tumble toward the darkness comes away with an unmistakable vision of the destiny of the eternal flesh. Possessed Evangelicals are not alone in awaiting *the rapture* of actual bodies floating upward like gas balloons. Opposition to cremation by many, if not most, conventional Christians and some Jews rests exactly on the grounds that the disembodied (or perhaps more accurately *deskeletalized)* soul will be lost at the time of resurrection. Some years ago a friend whose mate died in Paris found himself subject to a stern lecture from the supposedly secular officials at the Père-Lachaise cemetery and crematorium: "You understand he will be completely gone," they warned.

Nowhere have I found the presence of the dead as diminished physical beings so strong as in Naples, where I visited often in the 1990s. There the only slightly veiled pagan worship and praying over the bones of the dead has been a point of struggle with Vatican orthodoxy for centuries, and at least half a dozen chapels still hold great collections of skeletal parts. Women dressed in black descend regularly into the subbasements of the chapels to choose their own particular bones and then pray for the unknown souls presumed still to be attached to them. Others go daily to the great subterranean catacombs where the unknown victims of plagues and wars rest. Mothers, wives, and sisters of the recently dead trek out to the city's cemeteries each year and ask the undertakers to exhume the corpses of their lost ones so that they may bathe the remains and rewrap the shrouds that cover the desiccating corpses until the last creamy humidity ceases to ooze from the bones. Conservation of the bones is seen, one scholar of Renaissance church practice told me, as the visceral union of the physical and the numinous. By praying for their loved ones' release from purgatory, the penitent prayer-giver begs as well for his—though more often her—physical salvation as well. At the same time, the act of touching the remains of one who had already passed but would—or could—be resurrected gives to the penitent a visceral affirmation of the unity of the sacred and the profane, of the temporal and the eternal. She touched in order that she might be touched and thereby raised up.

The relationship between soul—or in modern language, consciousness—and body at the resurrection occupied no less a mind than the seventeenth-century British philosopher John Locke, credited as an intellectual forbear to Voltaire and Rousseau. In a relatively little-known exchange with the bishop of Worcester Edward Stillingfleet, Locke argued forcefully against any idea of a singular eternal body. Both rationalist and a believer, Locke wrote to the bishop that "at the last Day, when all Men are raised, there will be no Need to be assured of any one particular Man's Resurrection." Locke was among the first to identify *being* with *consciousness* rather than physicality. He went further: "there can from the Nature of things, be no Absurdity at all, to suppose, that the same Soul may, at different times be united to different Bodies." The soul, reunited with the all-encompassing nature of divinity, might find its expression at any moment throughout eternity in a seemingly infinite variety of human forms.

The bishop was aghast. Locke, a devout Christian, had opened the door to an infinite tunnel of reincarnation.

Everything that his church—the Anglicans—and the old mother church—the Vatican—had preached and everything depicted in the sacred illustrations of the Last Judgment would be turned upside down. More precisely, to follow Locke's logic, the soul could be aligned only to the newly emergent (and also anciently Platonic) idea of consciousness by which men and women had known themselves on earth. Locke's argument struck the bishop as a direct rejection of Jesus's second corporal visit to the disciples when he spoke to the doubting apostle, Thomas:

> Bring your fingers here and see my hands,
> And bring you hand and put it in my side,
> And do not be without faith but of faith.

Plainly the Jesus in chapter 20 of the book of John had appeared as he had last been on earth, his hands and feet pierced by the nails, his side slashed by a spear. Was this not evidence enough that those who were rewarded with eternal salvation would carry with them the flesh of the earth? Not at all, answers Locke, because the motive and function of Christ's appearance was to reinforce the faith of Thomas, which in itself was as immaterial as his soul. The son of God materialized himself in human form only so that humans constrained by their material limitations could see and believe and thereby reinforce the faith that would lead to the salvation of their souls.

Exotic as this seventeenth-century theological reasoning might strike the modern agnostic, it was and remains a core debate among philosophers and spiritual practitioners concerned with what generally gets subsumed under the mind/body problem. Though the mind/body conundrum goes back at least to Plato and Aristotle, who differed sharply on the relationship between the form of the soul and its relation to the form of the body, Catholics, and Dominicans especially, usually draw on their theological ancestor, Thomas Aquinas. Aquinas—in part 1, questions 76 through 89—reasoned that our "personhood" must include our physical bodies. Without the body and its sensorial capacity, the soul lacks memory and, by definition, physical perception: color, touch, smell, sound, taste. All these come from our physical learning, and when the purely earthly physical dimension shuffles away, the soul or spirit loses all those capacities. But Aquinas doesn't stop there.

Intellect, or mind, like soul, is separate from our physical bodies: eating, drinking, making love, defecating. But the habit of intellect, the repeated process of thinking derives both from our physical sensations—what we see and feel—and from our innate condition as humans. Intellect has a double source. And it abides in the untouchable spirit. As a result, says Aquinas, "Knowledge, therefore, acquired in the present life does not remain in the separated soul, as regards what belongs to the sensitive powers, but as regards what belongs to the intellect itself, it must remain." The body of the afterlife, in Aquinas's cosmology, loses its sense ability and its sense memory. It neither eats nor drinks nor enjoys orgasm. Even less does it comprehend those acts that its disappeared sense body experienced, and as a result it cannot comprehend the physical acts of those left among the living. Only pure mental comprehension persists.

An austere notion of being, we on the all-too-sensual earth might protest. But then that desensualized quality of being is what ascetics of the great religions have always sought (and what many maintain they have found in the total "disappearance" produced in Dionysian ritual).

On our last encounter, which retained both its sensual and its intellectual dimensions, Brother Peter and I caught up on several weeks of mutual journeys. Brother Peter was preparing for a number of preaching expeditions, one back to Africa and another to South America. One journey was to visit a convent of sisters, which in itself struck me as surprising until he reminded me that only priests are permitted to perform the offices of the Mass, and only men are permitted to be priests. Just as the eternal body had claimed our attention on the previous visit, *purity* emerged as our concluding topic.

He also spoke to me about his growing role as a counselor to a troubled younger priest with whom he had spent the morning. He had officiated at the younger priest's ordination, and the younger man had asked Brother Peter to continue as his spiritual father.

"Spiritual *father*?" I responded, suspiciously.

"Yes, his counselor."

"And this younger man, this younger priest doesn't know that his spiritual father is gay?"

"I don't think so; it's never come up."

"So he doesn't understand your physical appetites?"

"No, no, that wouldn't enter into this kind of relationship. Certainly not. When I am with someone for this sort of spiritual guidance, I cannot impose questions of that sort. Otherwise I would no longer have the distance or the necessary clarity. Now and then that could be a little difficult because the person before me can sense certain things, but if that happened, you must say honestly, 'I cannot continue. I'm not the right person to accompany you on your journey.'"

"It would put the purity of your spiritual duty at risk?"

"Exactly. You cannot do that."

We moved on to another encounter he had booked for the evening with an airline steward whom he hadn't seen for quite some time. That brought a blush of expectation, but it was purity I wanted to ask about, and it was more than clear that "purity" was not part of either Peter's or the steward's agenda.

All through our conversations Brother Peter was very clear that while he didn't carry particular guilt about his sexual life, he looked forward to a time when he wouldn't need sex and could fulfill his vows more purely. And then again, when we touched on the question of the form of eternal life, he spoke of purity. For Saint Augustine the earthly body of man was definitionally "impure" since it is born of the necessary but "impure" act of sexual copulation. Certainly to both Augustine and to the Dominican Thomas Aquinas the sex Brother Peter had had with me and with other men were purely "impure" acts, but did they threaten the "purity" of his being?

An act, sexual or otherwise, whose only motivation and function was to instrumentalize another person, was surely impure. But an impure act, as even the most conservative Vatican theologians including Pope Benedict have written, is not synonymous with an "impure being." The journey to salvation concerns beings—souls—and not acts.

A tricky slope, that. Were our souls not corrupted by the acts we committed? Were the SS agents who slaughtered six million, or for that matter the hired guards who tortured innocent civilians at Abu Ghraib, not engaging in the most impure of acts, and did those acts have no bearing on their being? Neither he nor I would of course assert equivalence between two men joined in ecstatic coitus and organized genocide, but within the eschatology of his faith, did that church's own definition of corruption and impurity not carry consequences to the soul of the actors?

For Aquinas, ever dedicated to Aristotelian reasoning, purity was not so important as its inverse: corruption. Human personhood exists as a species of nature that requires both soul and sense. If the soul without sensation is not a person, then the eternal soul, he argued, is not *necessarily* corrupted by the senses however errant they may be ("it is evident that human knowledge is not corrupted through the corruption of the subject for the intellect is an incorruptible faculty"). But knowledge can become corrupted either through false memory or through faulty argument contrary to the knowledge of nature according to Thomistic reasoning. Even so, however, the soul, which is incapable of memory once divided from its body, cannot retain the memory of corrupted intellect.

The arguments are intricate and highly parsed, as is all metaphysical reasoning. But finally the return to Aquinas led me to a better appreciation of Brother Peter's response to my much simpler question about what sort of "body" he expected to carry into eternity. Would it be, I pressed him, his current, still-attractive, middle-aged body, its hair thinning and the scar and limp of an earlier accident plainly apparent? Or would it be the hearty body he held as a young athlete? His answer seemed both to embrace Aquinas and to reject him.

"Jesus and the apostles have told us that when we join God we will be free of the corruptions of the world, and that means as well the corruptions of the flesh that has made us human in this world. The wear, the abuses, the tears, and decay that our bodies undergo are nothing but the corruptions of what we were at our most pure."

"Then your resurrected body would be as a newborn infant?"

"No. The infant, while he has a soul, is not yet a complete person. The soul while united in life to the body is informed and grows in its partnership with the senses even though it will leave the senses behind."

"But if it has left the quality of the senses on earth, then it cannot see, it cannot touch or feel, and the notion of the radiant perfect body ascending makes no sense."

"Perfection is not purity."

At which point he referred me to the "uncorrupted" bodies of the saints, exhumed, he said, after hundreds of years and yet still fresh and supple.

"You can find them on the internet. Look for yourself."

"Peter [increasingly I couldn't say *Brother Peter*], you can't be serious. You don't believe those stories?"

"But they're true. Medical doctors have been present at the exhumations and have certified that the skin of Saint Bernadette of Lourdes was soft to the touch and as pink as a flower forty-five years after she died. Her eyes were still clear."

I didn't know what to say. It seemed impossible that a worldly, educated man in or out of "the cloth" could be so credulous.

"The freshness of their flesh was the sign of their purity, of their incorruptibility," he said.

Here at this point in our concluding exchanges, most of my friends, and indeed most readers, may be ready to toss in the rosary. To be "of faith" is one thing. To cite flimsy declarations concerning the "uncorrupted bodies of the saints" is to lapse into fairy-tale thinking, and is surely, *ipso facto*, sufficient reason to dismiss Brother Peter as a creature of absurd anachronism. Indeed I myself had to ride down the temptation to ask him if in those moments when we were naked before God and the universe he felt himself as pure as these departed saints. It would have been a cheap retort to a certainly serious effort on his part to address the most mysterious of all human questions: What is our ultimate disposition? Whether he would carry with him for all time his young, wiry athlete's body or some far more degraded form was of no moment.

Aquinas wrote that whatever form the eternal spirit might take, having been cut off from the temporal flesh, it would have neither memory nor knowledge of corporal sensation. Body would have no meaning. Having no meaning, corporal desire would be nonsensical. Unlike John Locke, who insisted that the eternal spirit, being at one with God, would have the capacity to assume any and all forms at any and all moments, for Aquinas the eternal spirit would simply be incomprehensible to us terrestrial mortals. The "uncorrupted flesh" of the exhumed saints—from Italy's Padre Pio de Pietrelcina who died in 1968, to Saint Francis Xavier who departed in 1552 and others much older—was not so much a promise that "clean living" would guarantee a fit body in the next realm as it was a mark of the peacefulness that, in Brother Peter's view, attended their departure from the earth. The purity of soul that he sought was not a release from natural and human biological need, but instead from an internal spiritual deficit that desire in itself could not fulfill. To be released from those compulsions of desire, biologically linked to the imperative to preserve the species (even when desire expresses itself in nonprocreative directions), was to arrive at a state of pure spiritual contentment of *no knowledge* (as the Buddhists would have it) of the physical corpus and its ongoing, inevitable corruption and decay. To be fully free.

The official church's claims about their perfectly preserved saints might well be not only patently absurd (and indeed there are any number of meteorological and soil science explanations for their physical conservation unusual as they may be), but those relics of "the uncorrupted" spoke to Brother Peter of something that is not absurd, not ridiculous. To be free of physical fear. To be free of the intolerable angst at the prospect of our own decay and biological "corruption." To be free of the all-encompassing duty of each member of the species to defend and procreate for the collective survival of all. There lies possibly the enormous gift as well as the terrible truth of homosexual desire, that appearing to exist outside the universal law of collective succession, it is the very fact of our outlying status that, as the mystical Neapolitans would have it, has granted us a special spiritual vision if we could only open ourselves to the way of seeing it.

Though I would never have wanted the life that Brother Peter has followed (and though before he felt called to that path himself, he could never have imagined such a life), our dialogues have led me steadily away from my initial perception of him as a man trapped within absurdity, following a medieval practice in a ridiculous and perverse religion. I come away from our engagements not at all converted to his path nor any less severe in my view of the bloody record of his church. But my view of his journey has changed. He is no more absurd than any of the rest of us, and the "corruptions" past and ongoing of the hierarchy that he serves are neither greater nor fewer than any of the other corrupted institutions I have served and followed in my own journeys. Surely the singular lesson of the twentieth century is that none of the utopian institutions and movements we have invented is, or can be, free of corruption. Perhaps worse, following the thought of Isaiah Berlin, the will to create utopian institutions contains in itself the unpurgeable seed of corruption. More than anything, my time with Brother Peter has pressed me to reflect more intensely on what his life has to say about the mystery of passage. Whether our exchanges and meditations transpired across the round table of my Paris apartment or along the silent canals of the north, the true text was never far from the visceral experience of passage.

Canals have very often provided me apt locations for such reflections, as they did from time to time in this project. Canals are passages that consume time. To stroll along beside them sharing their silence is to be lost on the plain between the temporal and the terminal. Unlike lost roads in the forest that speak of human activity eaten by time, or rivers that flow from the birth of a spring to the oblivion of the sea, ancient canals and the paths that line them bring us into an intimation of time without time. A nearly still ripple captures the crimson of an opening tulip, a fragment of clover drifts possessed neither of purpose nor destination. As much as the duty of the canal is to offer passage, the tube of water in itself lies only in its own motionless moment, coming from nowhere, going nowhere.

Never mind the all-too-easy pop-Freudian erotic imagery that canals invoke, we are surely born with a sublime sense of the human body as an elemental canal. Yes, of course, we arrive by canal and we are thereafter only digestive canals evolved from biological ancestors who sucked in their nutrients from the floor of the sea and left behind new nutrients for the fish and the bivalves that were to come. Greater yet, however, is the notion that would have seemed far more familiar to Locke. As Lockean persons we are nothing but a vast network of canals through which flow the force of physical life and yet even with those smaller and smaller canals irrigating the flesh there are still lesser canals, the neurological pathways, through which the persistent currents of sensations crackle and flow. Even finer than those tiny canals of sense lie the all but invisible filaments through which pass the synaptic bursts of energy we call comprehension. Locke, the experimental materialist, would have taken delight in delving through all these canals of perception had he then possessed the means, yet in his greater spiritual perception, they all formed, network within network, the atomistic lineage of consciousness, and consciousness no more now than then remains the untouchable animator whose origins we do not know, whose destination we dream about, and whose force uses our all-too-fragile flesh as nothing but a temporary vessel.

That the vessel finally collapses? Yes, of course. Ultimately the only interesting question is what we make of the vessel. For Brother Peter the vessel that is his body has served him as an instrument of exploration and greater knowledge: as an athlete, as a teacher, as a man of passionate sensation, as a listener, confessor, and perceiver of a conscious force beyond himself. Unlike many thousands of his coreligionists, he chose not to deny and repress the physical and spiritual signals that were given to him, but instead to explore and comprehend them within the framework of consciousness he also found. Dominican theology at its best would advise only that it was his duty as a child of nature to do no less; indeed, to have done less would surely have constituted an act of bad faith, which is in Thomistic doctrine the only action that leads to the corruption of the soul.

Our passage together, the monk and the skeptic, concluded as quietly and reflectively as it had begun in that grand art gallery of painted photographs displaying the nearly naked bodies of the apostles nailed to rough, rugged crosses. I had gone to the gallery several months earlier, curious to see how outrageously kitsch the work would be, supposing as well that there might be other appealing visitors at the gallery. Instead I ended up meeting Brother Peter, who both enriched my perception of the artwork and led me into a half year of spiritual reflection that I would never have imagined undertaking. As I walked Brother Peter to the elevator on our final visit, I gripped his leather-clad shoulder, searching for the right words.

"Bon voyage," I said.

"And you, too," he answered.

1/30